AF611365

Real Talk: Navigating Critical Decisions in College and Beyond

Unveiling Secrets to Thrive at Life

Ali Qasim

Copyright © 2024 Q Publishing

All rights reserved.

Edition 2.1

ISBN: 9798334071230

CONTENTS

INTRODUCTION

This book is geared towards anyone who wants to be successful in life—the people who want to win.

If you're reading this book it already means you're already a dynamo in the making. If you have the hunger, the drive, and the determination to thrive and you will eventually get there.

My goal in writing this book is to provide you with knowledge to help you make wiser decisions with confidence during critical junctures of your life. Making the right decisions early on will pay you major dividends down the road in your life's journey. You can make rookie mistakes and still be successful, but the objective of this book is to provide you with a prescriptive level of knowledge so you avoid those mistakes in the first place—whether you're in high school, college or starting out in your working career.

There are some topics in this book that someone in their teens or early 20s may not find useful or interesting at the moment, but I promise they're important nuggets of knowledge you should be learning in high school. Today's education system teaches you how to follow commands and do a job, but not about navigating major life decisions and achieving financial success in the long-term. Financial literacy is an under-taught concept, but knowledge of the area can set you far ahead (or behind) based on how much you know and understand about that part of the world.

When it's time to make any critical life decision, you should never find yourself guessing with limited knowledge. A better understanding of financial concepts and career economics early on in your life could make the difference of hundreds of thousands of dollars over the course of your working career and when you retire.

I've spent more than 10 years working in a plethora of professional environments in the consulting space and more. The topics of conversation in this book are something I wish someone had told me when I was younger. I made a ton of mistakes related to investing, educational decisions, life, romance, and more due to lack of experience. My path to success was not straightforward, but the lessons learned from experiencing failure were instrumental to my success.

For most people it's not a straightforward path, but large deviations from the path to success you have planned in your head can cause a gargantuan amount of stress and anxiety when trying to forge a new path. I had numerous large deviations on my path—to the point that I got gray hair in my late 20s and I started balding from the stress. I figured out my path and am extremely happy with a lovely wife, beautiful daughter and a home (the grays and balding remain – I'm working on it). I want to help you minimize the amount of large deviations you take on your path, so you experience less stress/anxiety and your grays come in hopefully decades later than mine did.

Please note that I am pretty much a straight shooter. You may notice how blunt I am throughout this book. I promise I don't mean to offend anyone with the verbiage in this book and I apologize if I do in advance. I just want to speak to the reader as an older sibling would—straight to the point without the **BS** and bring you some laughs along the way. For those of you who like taking notes there's writing space near the end of the novel.

<u>Key Vocabulary:</u>

BS: Bullshit

PBS: Partial Bullshit

1

HARD WORK OVER LUCK

Susie looks across the restaurant and sees her high school crush, Jake, walking through the door as he proceeds to ask for a table. She hasn't seen Jake in more than 10 years—since high school. Susie smiles as she sees Jake.

But her excited smile turns into worry once she realizes Jake is going to ask her what she's been up to since high school. They were honors classmates together and she was a straight A student. What if he asks her why she's still working as a waitress at a restaurant 10 years after high school? Through conversation, Susie finds out that Jake has a successful job as an engineer in New York. Shortly after, Jake says his goodbyes and joins his family in the waiting area.

Short story over. Here's the rub:

Many would feel bad for Susie. Poor Susie had some bad luck and couldn't take advantage of her talents after peaking in high school. The problem with that mentality is that luck is never a big portion of why people are successful. Jake didn't luck his way into an engineering degree. Michael Jordan and Kobe Bryant didn't luck themselves into the NBA. They worked hard, dedicated themselves to their craft, and made intelligent decisions. If anyone told me I got where I am today simply because of luck I would honestly be insulted.

You don't want to be in a similar position as Susie in your 30s working multiple minimum wage jobs to scrape by because you didn't make the right decisions in high school or college. In order for you to avoid Susie's situation you must make the right decisions in your teens and early 20s so you can set yourself up for success in the long-term. Your potential aspirations of a dream vacation, becoming a homeowner, starting a family, and more, would likely be delayed because your financial needs are not being met in this scenario.

The purpose of this book is to provide you with **BS**-free advice backed by data and experience to help you make better decisions so that your hard work and dedication can provide a better output for your future. You've probably heard the quote "It's better to be lucky than to be good.". In order for you to be in a position to be lucky you need to put in the hard work and dedicate yourself to your craft.

Working smart is important, but don't misinterpret that with shortcuts. Leaders, CEOs and hiring managers can tell the difference between someone who's actually put in the work to get to where they are today and someone who took shortcuts. They can understand that because they're the real deal – it takes one to know one 😊

2

INTELLIGENTLY FOLLOW YOUR PASSION

Throughout high school, college, and even workplace environments you may hear leaders and advisors counsel you to 'Follow your Passion' in the career world. Follow your passion and you'll be successful. I categorize this as **PBS (Partial BS).**

If you can follow your passion and be successful that's fantastic. For example, if you love crunching numbers and banking/accounting is your passion (and you're good at it), then you'll probably work hard during college and be successful because you enjoy the work. By successful I mean within five years of working experience (or sooner) have a salary of at least double the national salary average—that is about $100,000 annually (In the second quarter of 2023 approximately $50,000 was reported as the national salary average.)[1]. Normally, those making at least double the average salary will be able to pay average expenses (rent, food, student loans, etc.), contribute well into their retirement plan, and are able to save for a rainy-day fund (as long as they're being fiscally responsible).

Many others follow their passion in different career paths, but sadly their passions do not lead to financial success in the long-term. Selecting college majors with historically low-income prospects post-graduation does not jive with long-term financial success. This can be considered a low income passion. While they may be passionate about the subjects and graduate top of their class, they would have to generally be in the top 10% of their fields to truly do well and make a good salary. The cost of living has skyrocketed during the past 20 years and the American Dream is now in jeopardy. In 2022, the median sale price for a single-family home in the US was 5.6 times higher than the median household income, higher than at any point on record dating back to the early 1970s[2]. Salaries have not risen at close to the same rate.

Those pursuing careers in low-income passion generally

struggle to save money every month to pay average expenses (rent, food, student loans, etc.) and taking on high interest debt can unfortunately become an option to survive. Too much high interest debt can set you back from your financial goals for years. You want to be the one earning interest on your investment, not the one paying it to someone else via debt.

Life lesson: just because you're passionate about something doesn't mean you're good at it. If you don't believe me just record yourself singing your favorite song in the shower. Take a listen and you'll catch my drift. If this scenario doesn't apply then please go audition for *American Idol*.

The KEY TO SUCCESS here is to find out what you're good at that also provides a good income. You should definitely follow your passion, but maybe your passion shouldn't be a career choice. **You should follow your passion intelligently**. For example, my friend John is great at working with technology, but loves art. My friend Jacob is great at construction but is a history buff. My friend Jingleheimer would make a great engineer but is passionate about criminal justice. To round it out, friend Schmidt would make a great doctor, but loves journalism.

All four of my friends, John, Jacob, Jingleheimer, and Schmidt should all follow career paths in line with what they're good at and turn their passions into hobbies. For example, John could pursue a degree in technology, get a job in the field and use his higher salary to buy art or create his own art after work instead of becoming an art historian. He doesn't have to make his low-income passion into his career. Following your passion can equate to happiness, but it won't always work in your best interest to give you enough income for your version of the American dream.

Some of you may be wondering – what if John is the next Leonardo Da Vinci or the next Van Gogh? What if we miss the next Mona Lisa? Finding the next great artist like this is one in a million. Yes there is the one, but what about the 999,999 who failed? Do they have a backup plan or an ability to get back on the path to success and live out their interpretation of the American Dream? The odds are not in your favor – you're much better off pursuing your passion as a side hustle or hobby instead of making it a career choice. Like the Hunger Games, we would prefer for the "odds be ever be in your favor". If you pursue your passion as a side hustle and you start to see a path to pursuing your passion as a career then maybe make the transition. But have the foundation of a good paying career first so you have a fallback option.

Overall, you want a good ROI (return on investment) from your college degree. For example, if you invest in Apple's stock you expect your investment to appreciate (grow in value) over time and give you a good ROI. You have to look at college the same way: you're investing in a college degree so you can earn a well-paying job (or return) on the investment you made into your college degree.

Whether you take out student loans, obtain scholarships, or your parents are helping you with paying for college you want to make sure you're getting good value out of the expenditure. It's your parent's hard-earned money or it will be YOUR hard-earned money after graduation (plus interest). It may not be something that's as important to you now, but it will be not too far after graduation. Too much student loan debt can hold you back from purchasing a home, your dream car and more in the future depending on your situation.

COVID truly changed everything. The salaries of two teachers could raise a family and buy a home pre-covid. Post-pandemic two teachers would have a much rougher time achieving their dreams due to financial constraints. You'd be living month to month trying to own a home, raise kids and live the life you want.

Disclaimer: I promise I'm not trying to career-shame art historians or any others that follow low paying career paths. They're just not lucrative investments of your time, money, blood, sweat, and tears. Imagine graduating with an arts degree and having more than $100,000 in student loan debt only to find a job that barely pays the bills. It's just not practical. Degrees such as these are definitely needed in society, but I would not advise these career path if you want long term financial health for you and your family.

3

CRITICAL DECISIONS IN HIGH SCHOOL

High school is truly an exciting time in which you're still figuring yourself out and you're in the early stages of preparing for adulting. You're likely living under your parents' roof and you're starting to slowly gain more independence over the years. With more autonomy comes more responsibility. The choices you make during high school may follow you into your college years and beyond. Fortunately, you're reading the right book to help you with those choices 🙂

Finding a Career Path/Picking a Major

Now that we've discussed following your passion intelligently, the next step would be to find a career path that in which you're proficient and would give you a good ROI for your college degree. Careers in STEM (science, engineering, technology and math) medicine, business, law, finance and many more will generally land you in a great financial position after college.

It's possible some of your high school friends may call you a nerd (or worse) for taking more advanced classes in order to align better with your potential major or even obtain college credits in high school. It's very important for you to play chess and not checkers at this point in time. You need to play the long game. Generally, in order to beat intermediate or better players at chess you have to think five to ten moves ahead to trap the player into a check or checkmate. You can't let your classmate's comments or their perception of you get to your head and detract you from your goals. The way you perceive the world can lead to many great things, but worrying about Silly Sally's thoughts about your wardrobe isn't a constructive use of your time.

When you see your old classmate Karen (who used to annoy you) working as a Bartender in her 30s while you roll up in your Mercedes it'll all be worth it. And trust me it will happen—I have seen countless friends from high school in their 30s working as a bouncer, bartender or even flipping burgers at a fast-food restaurant. There's nothing wrong with these jobs for the short-term, but they should not end up being your long-term career. Don't let your bullies improve your chances of turning your future self into a loser in your 30s. In all honesty, I feel their pain and wish they had someone to guide them in the right direction earlier in their lives.

High school is important, but as soon as you start college you'll be in a new environment making new friends and having new experiences. Being a popular kid in high school should never be your ultimate goal—preparing yourself for college and the real world is much more important. Enjoy your time in high school, but know there's a bigger world for you to conquer outside the HS bubble.

During career research you should look into the following criteria:

- Actual jobs that align with your potential career path.
- The number of available jobs and rates of employment.
- Longevity of the job position (for instance, could the role be replaced by AI?).
- Long-term career growth, salary and positional advancement.

Choosing your Major

Let's be honest: most college students change their major during their college journey. Approximately 80% of college students change their major at least once[3]. However common it may be, changing your major can cause some or all of your courses to be a waste of time and money. The courses you take for one major may not be required for a different major causing you to take more courses to satisfy requirements of the new major. In order to minimize the likelihood of changing your major let's take some time to actually align on some potential career paths.

Disclaimer: If you choose a major and find out that you absolutely cannot spend your career doing this day in and day out (for whatever reason) then DEFINITELY change course. You don't want to be working in a career that you dislike for the next 30 years and then pass on those stresses onto your loved ones over time—that's no bueno.

When people are stressed about work they may inadvertently take out that stress on their loved ones—straining the relationship. Becoming too stressed about work can also be draining to your mental health. Mental health is another form of wealth. If you can't find a major that you enjoy, then you'd be better off choosing a major that leads to work that's tolerable for you. Either way that major must provide a solid income for you in the long term.

It's very possible that earnings are not a key driver in your motivations for a college degree. Many people choose career paths without keeping income in mind which is completely understandable. It's possible they have alternative forms of income that supplements their day job or that they're simply not thinking about it when they should. After graduation they stick it out a few years on the job to realize it's hard to get by month to month and that long-term their opportunity for salary increases in their industry may be minimal. The only options left at that point are starting over in a new industry, sticking it out or going back to school.

My wife experienced this first-hand. She has a degree in the field of education, but now works in digital marketing. She spent more than nine years in the education industry before switching to marketing. She worked with countless members of staff in education who had numerous years of experience but were unhappy with the salary and workplace environment. They loved the kids, but they were struggling to pay their bills. Many started looking for work in other industries or even had to take on a second job in order for their family to meet their financial needs. I would highly recommend keeping an open mind and at least learning more about what you're getting yourself into so you can make more informed decisions about your future.

Medical School

If you're thinking about medical school after graduation PLEASE come up with a solid backup plan or option. Getting into medical school is pretty tough and you may have to obtain additional degrees after your bachelor's if you don't get into medical school and you're dead set on that career path. If you wish to pursue this option to become a doctor please understand the potential length of school to finish as part of this journey:

- Four years of undergrad;
- Four years of medical school;
- Up to seven years of residency; and
- Then up to another three years of fellowship.

That could equate to a whopping 18 years of college, residency and fellowship depending on whether you specialize or opt for general practice—and bear in mind that tuition get more expensive after undergrad. The average medical student has more than $250,000 in student loan debt[4]. Medical school dropout rates are between 16% and 18%[5]. That's around 1 in 6 medical students. Imagine taking on medical school debt and you drop out. You're stuck with student loan debt for a degree you didn't even finish, and you have to go back to school to find a good paying job to pay it all back along with new tuition costs.

During residency, pay is abysmal and hours are long. Average base salary for a medical resident is $59,314[6] and a 2018 National Resident Survey showed that a majority of residents work more than 60 hours a week and one in five worked more than 80 hours a week.

To make it worse, over half the residents experienced symptoms of burnout[7]. Typically, you would at least be around your early to mid 30s before you start getting paid 'like a doctor'. The average salary for physicians in primary care is $260,000 and specialty care is $368,000[8]. Sure—the salary when you finish your 11-18 years of training might be fantastic, but is this worth the sacrifice you'd have made in your 20s? Your available time to find a partner, travel, and just 'enjoy life' would have been limited significantly and if you're not able to have these life experiences in your 20s, how would it be possible with up to $250,000 of debt? Maybe you can make it work, but that debt could be weighing you down for decades while you try to buy a house, get married, have a kid, buy a car, and so on.

Some of you may receive pressure from family members to pursue this path (or other paths) for the prestige or to follow the footsteps of your parents. When it comes to medical school if your heart's truly not in it you're much less likely to be successful and you could put yourself in a bad position mentally. There's a reason why medical students are three times more likely to die of suicide and about 27%[9] of medical students worldwide experience depression[26]. There's intense duress in medical school and potentially pressure to make your parents proud. If your heart and mind isn't in it, I would advise you to choose an alternative path and you'll be more likely to find happiness over time.

The reason for pessimism here is that if you truly want to go in this direction you must be fully committed and have a plan. You must be at peace with the sacrifice you're making to get to where you want to go and be absolutely determined in your path to get there. It MUST be your number one priority for more than a decade of your life.

If I didn't scare you away by this point then maybe you're cut out to go the medical school route 😊

Business School

Business school can be a great option if you're passionate about business or need an alternative because your true passion doesn't give a lucrative return on investment. There will always be a need for people in business, but it's not something exclusive to just those with business degrees. For example, you have to pass certification exams after college to be a nurse in a hospital. You don't need a certification after college to work a business-related job at a Fortune 500 company. Many pivot to business related jobs in their careers and they don't have business degrees. A business degree will give you a leg up ahead of the competition, but there are additional learnings you need to take action upon to be successful in this area.

First of all, "if you wanna be a duck you have to walk, talk, act, quack and dress like a duck". What the hell does that mean?

When in grad school at Texas A&M University my favorite professor, Dr. Alexander, offered this advice to the class on the first day and—like you probably are—I was pretty confused. I presumed he was going to ask us all to get up and start quacking for a good grade. What he meant was if you want a certain job in the real world you need to start acting like you're already doing the job. If you want to be a hospital CEO you need to dress, walk, talk and act like a CEO. Smile when you talk to people and read up on the industry in your own free time. Be optimistic about the future of your industry. Think of this as an investment in yourself by building your base of knowledge when you talk to industry professionals.

Second, start reading books on business and public speaking so you can speak the lingo with folks who are in business. Communication is key in business and if you can't have a proper conversation and keep up with business conversation during an interview, you probably won't get the job. Alternative topics to read about could be how startups grew into prominent businesses and learning new and innovative processes or business tactics that are helping firms thrive in the modern era.

If you're in high school take a debate class as an elective. Joining high school debate completely transformed my ability and confidence to speak in public. We had many opportunities to speak to groups and practice speaking without fillers.

Third, make sure you network and talk to people. Ask those in management how they got their role and what they do on a day-to-day basis. Add them on LinkedIn after you meet with them. Building up your LinkedIn is an important part of long-term success. This will come in handy if you have trouble finding your first job or after you possibly get tired of your first job after graduation and want to try something new.

STEM (Science, Technology, Engineering, and Math), law, finance and more

These career areas will most likely always be needed for society to run and careers in these fields provide a good ROI in the long term. If you go into a non-physician medical profession I would advise you to look at the length of school required to gain your degree and the median pay scale for roles in that profession. There are also many other majors/career paths that provide great earnings long-term as well outside of what I have listed on the next page. Do your research extensively to make sure you're on the right path. Research prospective jobs and their median earnings/progression prospects to see if it's a fit for you.

The top 20 median earning majors after only a bachelor's degree are listed on the next page:

Median Earnings Per Major[10]	
Electrical Engineering	$110,000
Computer Engineering	$104,000
Pharmacy, Pharmaceutical Sciences, and Administration	$100,000
Chemical Engineering	$100,000
Computer Science	$100,000
Aerospace Engineering	$100,000
Materials Engineering and Materials Science	$98,500
Engineering Mechanics, Physics, and Science	$95,000
Mechanical Engineering	$95,000
Industrial and Manufacturing Engineering	$90,000
Physics	$90,000
Electrical Engineering Technology	$90,000
Petroleum Engineering	$90,000
General Engineering	$90,000
Management Information Systems and Statistics	$89,000
Civil Engineering	$89,000
Health and Medical Preparatory Programs	$87,000
Applied Mathematics	$85,000
Economics	$85,000
Transportation Sciences and Technologies	$85,000
Nursing	$70,000

Arts, Social Work, Education, Psychology, and Communications

If you're motivated for a high salary after graduation, majors in arts, social work, education, psychology, and communications may not be the best option. If one of these is your passion I would advise to pursue it as a hobby. Even if your significant other/spouse is wealthy or pursuing a highly paid career choice and would carry the financial load I would not recommend pursuing a lower paid profession. Relationships are not guaranteed to last, and you may need financial independence one day.

Median Earnings Per Major[10]	
Visual and Performing Arts	$35,000
Early Childhood Education	$43,000
Social Work	$48,000
General Education	$50,000
Counseling Psychology	$50,000
Art History and Criticism	$50,000
Communication Disorders Sciences and Services	$57,000
Educational Psychology	$60,000

These career choices are very important to society and are honestly underpaid. The problem is the demand and revenue opportunities for businesses with these groups are generally not very strong. I hope the average salary rises for these groups in the future as they're important to society.

Picking a College

Once you've narrowed down a major to pursue it's time to apply to various colleges. I have worked in consulting for more than 10 years, and the college I went to barely comes up in conversations anymore.

What's more important in the real working world is merit, communication, refining your craft, and building relationships consistently. With that being said it's still important to pick a good college, but if you have a choice between private and public I would advise to go the public route to save on tuition. On average, tuition from a four-year private nonprofit university is almost three times the cost of in-state tuition at a four-year public school; to be exact it's 282.4% higher than public tuition on average[11]. Imagine paying three times more for the same exact shoes just because of a brand name. Right now, is not the time for Louis Vuitton or Gucci; Nike and Adidas work just fine for this situation. You can buy yourself brand names bags or shoes with all your tuition savings down the road.

College can definitely help you get your foot in the door with some organizations, but that's not exclusive to a few select colleges. Most reputable institutions have resources to help you get a job after graduation. My point here is this: you should pick a reputable college for name brand recognition, but not so reputable that you're paying an arm and a leg in tuition every year. Think Texas A&M or the University of Texas instead of the University of Phoenix or St. Edwards College. Just about everyone in the state of Texas knows Texas A&M and the University of Texas. University of Phoenix isn't very credible and St. Edwards is not well known in state or national circles. The only exception to this rule to save on tuition costs would be if you got into an Ivy League school and/or a national top 10 or 15 school for your major. Many top-tier employers are willing to pay more salary for candidates from top colleges or top schools related to the job position to get the best talent. Some employers exclusively hire only from particular colleges annually. Every situation is different and you should make the right decision for yourself.

If you want to save even more on tuition or you have trouble getting into a reputable college there's absolutely no shame in going to community college for the first year or two. You can always transfer to a more reputable institution after taking community college courses. When applying for jobs you don't need to include the community college in your resume either. Just include where you received your bachelor's degree. I highly doubt any prospective employer would ask—and even if they did I'm not sure how much it would matter. All you need to include is where you graduated from and the degree you received.

For the love of God, please do not pick a college solely because:

- Your significant other is going there;
- Your siblings, parents, cousins or friends went there;
- You're tired of living at home and you want to get away;
- You'll have a roommate to live with;
- They have your favorite sports team; or
- It's 'prestigious, reputable, distinguished or respected' (unless it falls within the exception stated earlier in the chapter).

This is a key moment in your life in which you need to do what's best for you and only you. That's it.

NOBODY ELSE.

I can't tell you how many horror stories I've heard about living with your best friend or someone following their boyfriend to their college. Most of my colleagues—myself included—are barely friends with their high school classmates in our 30s. That's because you'll likely meet double (at the minimum) the amount of people in college and the working world than what you met in high school. College is your opportunity to carry your learnings from high school and start fresh with new people.

Nobody in college is going to know or remember your loud fart in gym class or your stumble on the high school graduation stage. Take the opportunity for new beginnings and capitalize on your opportunities.

What criteria should you consider to choose a college to attend?

- Tuition costs;
- Scholarship opportunity;
- Aligns with your major and is ranked decently at the minimum for your career path;
- Brand name recognition (to an extent)
- Cost of living;
- Facilities; and
- Size.

Hot Tip: making decisions in life is hard and data can help you get there. Jeff Bezos (former CEO and Founder of Amazon) would famously coach his management teams to get 70% of the data they thought they needed for a specific decision. When you have 70% of the data you think you need, you should go ahead and make your decisions with the data you have. If you wait until you feel like you've obtained 90-100% of the data you'll be too slow and honestly just stress yourself out even more with the process[12]. This may not apply to ALL situations but may be helpful for certain ones.

4

SUCCEEDING IN COLLEGE

You've made a decision on a major and which college to attend. Congratulations! Your hard work has brought you to the next step in your life and career. The topics I cover in this chapter are areas of focus mostly outside of maintaining good academic standing and getting good grades.

Tips for Getting Good Grades:

Try listening to classical music like Mozart or Beethoven while you study. See if it's helpful over your normal no-noise routine or listening to your favorite music while you study. A USC study showed that classical music benefits the brain, sleep patterns, the immune system and stress levels which are all important while studying for exams[13].

It's important to maintain a balance between partying and studying but prioritize studying first. I know I sound like a parent, but there will always be more parties. Don't let the FOMO (fear of missing out) of missing a party get to you. If you skip studying for an exam and you fail, the FOMO from not studying will be much worse.

Student Loans

Money. Money. Money.

Money can't buy you happiness in the long-term, but it can definitely bring you some peace of mind and financial security. Financial education is key to your success. Earning money is one part of the equation, but actually saving and investing your money correctly is what builds long-term wealth.

Student loans can be a huge hindrance to your financial success long-term. Take the LEAST amount of student loans possible to be successful. Take time during high school/college to look for scholarships. Be responsible with your student loan dollars—don't forget you have to pay it back plus interest. Apply for federal aid and see what options are presented to you based on your situation. If your parents make over a certain income you probably won't get too much in federal aid for college. Discuss with your parents how to best handle this financial burden. Are they able to support you in your college journey or is this going to be solely your responsibility? Your parents might want to help you, but if they don't have the financial flexibility it may not be possible. If federal aid is not an option, your next steps are hoping that your parents have an educational savings account for you, then applying for scholarships, and finally—sadly—exploring student loan options.

You should consider subsidized loans over unsubsidized loans. Federally subsidized loans are loans where the federal government will pay the interest on the loans until you graduate. Unsubsidized loans will build interest as soon as you take the loan. Unsubsidized interest will compound and grow your balance much larger than what you initially took out by the time you graduate.

After graduation, instead of saving for a better car, home, or putting more dollars in my retirement account early-on I was stuck paying off my student loans. Here and there if you wanna live it up and enjoy life as a student honestly you should—but set a budget and be responsible. You may think that you'll be making good money after graduation and you can pay for it, but taxes and basic expenses generally turn out to be higher than our estimated budgets. If you're borrowing money you will want to pay the least amount of interest possible, especially if interest is unsubsidized and going to accumulate on the loan over the period you're in school. Private student loans should be a LAST resort; Sallie Mae ain't your friend (it's a private student loan servicing company).

All in all, if you can pick a college that has an affordable tuition cost and you're able to minimize student loans as much as possible you'll be setting yourself up to be in a great financial position post-graduation.

Friendships

Friendships are important in college and, if you're an extrovert, you'll naturally make a wide variety of friends over time. The friends you keep around you will end up influencing you in many different directions. It's important that they nudge you in the right direction and not negatively influence you towards blowing off classes or doing drugs.

Don't worry about winning the popularity contest in college. If you fall out with one crowd, just find another. You may have some friends from high school attending the same college as you. Stay in touch with them if you like them, but I'd recommend that you eventually venture out and meet new people. Join a club and socialize; get out of your comfort zone. You will never get your 20s back. Minimize your regret and go enjoy your time at college (within reason 😉).

Your close friends during freshman year of college may not be the same as your junior year. Over time you'll meet new people and find out what you're truly looking for in terms of a friend. Some friends will turn out to be toxic. Some will just use you for your resources. Unless there's a good trade off you'll hopefully learn to avoid these people and find good friends you can rely on.

Roommates

Becoming friends with your roommate will have its peaks and valleys. You'll have someone to go places with you, but if you have a falling out or they start to get annoying you're taking that drama home with you. It would be ideal that you don't crap where you sleep. You should be cordial, respectful, have a good relationship with your roommates, but take it slow before becoming besties with them. It could take weeks or months before you see the real side of your roommates. Do they clean after dinner? Do they leave their dinner dishes in the sink for you to clean? Do they mix their laundry with yours or borrow your stuff without asking? If they're freshman it's likely this is the first time they're living away from their parents.

Create some ground rules between yourself and your

roommates to ensure things stay clean and cordial. Start a group chat to stay connected. You want your home to your place of peace and not a war zone. Especially if you bring home a hot date and she can smell yesterday's pasta in the living room.

Not a good look bro.

<u>Relationships</u>

When it comes to relationships you'll probably meet many people that you find attractive. I'm sure you've heard from your friends that college is your time to try new things and let loose. It's good to explore, go on dates, and have new experiences, but if you meet the one, try and take it seriously. I know there's plenty of fish in the sea, but finding true love is one in a million. During college you're constantly in classes and activities that automatically put you around many romantic prospects. After college that automatic social life vanishes. The number of prospects you see during everyday activities declines and you'll have to look via less traditional methods like dating apps, work organizations, or clubs/bars. That's not to say you can't find someone after college, but your likelihood of finding good prospects does start to diminish as you get older.

I met my wife at 27 through a dating app and we got married two years later. She is truly the one in a million match for me and I do not regret any of the decisions I made relationship wise prior to meeting her. None of the women I dated before her ever had the same level of compatibility, trust, beauty, thoughtfulness and loyalty that she does. If you're an ex and reading this—sorry it is what it is (LOL). You can find love after college as we did, but there will be many opportunities to find your love in college as well. Your soulmate might be on a jog right now on your college campus—keep your eyes peeled 😉.

One key benefit of finding a partner in college is that you'll have more time to figure each other out and potentially start living together earlier. You can unlock the golden key of the 21st century—you can be DINKs for longer. DINK = Double Income No Kids.

Failure

Failure is pivotal to success throughout life. Generally, you'll have the most failure early on in your life, but you have to keep failing forward. You're probably thinking this guy keeps talking about thriving at life in this book and he's asking us to fail. The key to this is to actually learn from your failures. Failing forward means you need to view failures as opportunities for growth and improvement. If you keep failing at something, but you don't take the time to mentally decompress and understand why you failed, it's much more likely the failure will occur again. You need to take time to understand why you failed and take action towards it.

If you didn't make a good impression during an interview, take the time to actually debrief afterwards. If a date didn't go so well maybe you just weren't their type. Or maybe they didn't like your manners or your style. All of this takes practice, but that doesn't mean you can't Google some dating tips.

I know many people that wake up at 7am to journal their thoughts and debrief the previous day. Journaling can help reduce stress, achieve goals, improve communication, and find inspiration[25]. I know it may sound lame, but you need to think about your own mental wellbeing. Stop worrying about what others think about your actions. If I only thought about what others wanted I would have probably been an accountant like my parents wanted. Just because I'm good with numbers doesn't mean I want to do math my whole life.

The fear of failure is completely normal—you just have to come to terms with failure and think about the long-term. You may have some failures in the short term, but you and your peers likely won't remember them 10 years later when things truly count. Let's imagine you're 18 years old and you make a critical mistake your first week of college. I can promise you nobody is going to remember the mistake within a month and within a year you'll have forgotten about it yourself.

You also can't be afraid of failure. Be bold! Be confident! But if you're wrong you're wrong. Own it and learn from it. Every time you're wrong you'll keep getting better and be less likely to fail again in the future if you fail forward. If you fall during a dance at a wedding everyone will forget within the hour. But it's very likely you're going to take necessary steps during the next dance practice to ensure you don't fall again. Therefore, you'll be less likely to fall during your next dance performance.

Networking

Throughout college you'll have countless opportunities to meet people, socialize, and have a grand ole time. You'll meet people at parties, classes, conferences, clubs, and orientations. You'll make new friends over time and maybe even some lifelong besties. One thing you need to take advantage of at this critical time in college is networking.

I'm sure you'll hear professionals advising you to network over and over again. Network and you'll find a job. What you don't hear is what you should do after you meet someone who works at a company you'd like to work for or someone you think is smart and will probably do big things one day.

First of all, you need to set up your professional socials—not Facebook or Instagram—make sure you have a LinkedIn profile.

Find a professional photo of yourself solo (no solo cups included) and update your profile. Don't wait until you start applying for internships or jobs to create a LinkedIn profile. Some employers do advanced research and will notice. Add everyone you know on LinkedIn. Doesn't matter whether they're in your industry or not. The mutual connections could come in handy someday. When two people realize there's a mutual connection it can create trust and potentially a talking point during conversation.

When you meet people at events in college remember to write their name down in your notes app on your phone and add them later on LinkedIn. I know that may sound a little creepy but hear me out. This gets you into the practice of building your network while you're in college. At this stage of your life, you're going to have a high level of social interactions automatically. Take advantage of them. When you start work you'll have the opportunity to network with those at work, but you'll have to actually go out of your way to network with people who don't work with you. Here you have a built-in connection machine that you can take advantage of now. These connections will help you greatly once you actually go into the working world. Also please note that LinkedIn is not the place to 'slide into the DMs'. It does not go down in those DMs.

After graduation you'll see LinkedIn updates for those who are starting new roles. If you're struggling to find a position, use the connections you made in the past to forge a new future for yourself.

Maybe you do find a job after college, but after a few years you find a job at Microsoft that would just be a dream fit for your skills and your wallet. You just happen to have a connection from college who already works there and can refer you.

In conclusion, the concept is to start building your LinkedIn network of connections earlier so that you have more connections to help you find new gigs when you need them. Alternatively, many companies do offer referral bonuses for referring good candidates. If you refer a candidate that gets hired you could receive a bonus for your referral worth hundreds or thousands of dollars depending on the company. Your connections could turn into a nice little referral bonus for you someday.

Side note: Elder folk may tell you to print business cards, but this is **BS.** The concept of business cards is outdated unless you're trying to network with senior citizens. Don't waste your money and focus on improving in other ways.

Internships

Internships are a key to success because it's a level above networking. You're actually working with people to showcase your skill set and build relationships with potential future colleagues or managers.

Here are six tips around the topic of internships:

1. Don't take an internship unless it's paid. Like my good friend Shanaly says: "That's not an internship, that's a volunteership." The only exception to this would be if it's your junior year and you haven't done an internship yet. If it's a good opportunity maybe you should accept the internship if you don't have any better offers. Hopefully if you do a good enough job it will translate into a job offer post-graduation.

2. Take the opportunity to add everyone you meet on LinkedIn and collaborate with your advisors/managers to meet with those who are working in the field in which you have interest. If they're not too helpful then look at the outlook directory and find people who work in departments that color you intrigued. Message them saying you're an intern and ask if they have 10 minutes to connect virtually. If you're in the office with them, ask if you can buy them a cup of coffee. More likely than not they won't let you buy them coffee (I mean you're an intern come on) and even if you do the connection could come in handy down the road if you do a good enough job. Think of it as an investment.

3. If there's a summit or happy hour with alcohol, stick to a two-drink limit. You gotta learn how to talk the talk before you walk the walk. If you nudge management the wrong way you'll likely

get put on the do not hire list. Trust me, they do have a do not hire list. Come up with good questions to ask people before the event—we have AI nowadays it shouldn't be that hard. Do your homework and you'll be rewarded down the road.

4. Check your emails and respond in a timely manner. You want to show management you're available and ready to work. Keep yourself organized; treat this like a real job and maybe they'll actually give you one.

5. Read your emails twice before you send them. Know when to reply vs reply all to an email. You don't want to be the person who replies all to the wrong email with sensitive information—it looks very unprofessional. Smile when you talk to people. Engage with them and be positive. Don't worry about what the other interns think. When you're first in line for the job it'll be worth the trouble.

6. Don't get it twisted—this is definitely a competition between yourself and the other interns. As a manager I can tell you—you will be reviewed and ranked internally on a hire list. You won't get a job offer just because you did the internship. Put in that extra effort and you'll be more likely to reap the benefits. Try to do an internship every summer you possibly can if it makes sense and especially if it's paid.

Fancy Big Name Companies vs Smaller Corporations

There are pros and cons to joining larger or smaller organizations. More likely than not you would encounter large and small organizations to have these attributes:

Larger Corporations:

Pros:

- Brand name appeal will help you land another role if needed down the road. Smaller and competing organizations will salivate to bring you aboard and absorb processes from the large company you came from.
- More likely to make your family prouder because they can brag to their family and friends that 'my son/daughter works at Lockheed Martin or McKinsey.
- Will likely be a pretty structured environment. Policies, procedures, etc., will likely be defined by the time you get there so you'll know the rules and how to follow them.
- Benefits and pay will probably be better than a smaller to medium organization. Potentially a 401k Match, better healthcare plans, company phone, reimbursement for using your personal phone for work, gym reimbursement, better professional development opportunities/etc.

Cons:

- It may be harder to get into these organizations as there will be more candidates applying to each role.
- Less opportunity to wear multiple hats and gain more experience. At larger organizations you may get siloed into a particular role. You may or may not like the role and will have to fight for the opportunity to take on more responsibility to get more experience.
- Less opportunity to create something new and bring change upon an organization. Larger corporations take a long time to accept and implement new policies or subdivisions.

Small to Medium Size Corporations

Pros:

- You'll likely have an opportunity to wear multiple hats and gain more professional experience than your colleagues in larger organizations. This will be beneficial when you're interviewing for your next role as you'll have more experience to discuss and bring to the table.
- You'll likely have an opportunity to work closely with professionals at higher levels of the organization such as a VP or Senior Manager. Observe how they operate and build a relationship. If they like you and they trust you, you'll be golden in the organization and set up for success if you work

hard. Build a mentorship relationship with someone else in management to gain information which could lead to an edge in your pursuit for a promotion or raise.

- They may be more flexible with work attire and remote working arrangements.

Cons:

- Brand name appeal may not be as strong
- Benefits and pay may not be as great compared to larger organizations.
- Your growth opportunities may be limited if there's not an opportunity for you to move up in the organization. There may be some level of management above you in the hierarchy that is very cozy in their role and not going anywhere anytime soon. Once you get to that point you'll naturally know when to start looking around due to lack of room for growth. If you're not sure, take a look at the company org chart and analyze where you're at and the levels above you.

Please keep in mind that these pros and cons above are generalities based on most organizations in their size bracket. There can be smaller organizations that pay as good as bigger organizations and bigger organizations that provide opportunities to wear more hats and gain more experience quickly. Apply to both and see where it takes you.

5

LANDING YOUR FIRST JOB

The process of finding a job can be tough, stressful, and feel like a job in itself. Filling out those old-school applications that don't parse your resume data can be annoying and time consuming. Interviewing can be stressful and potentially require homework before the interview. I know it's not fun, but you must treat finding a job like a job in itself. You're working for your own future—don't you want the best for you?

Over 97% of Fortune 500 companies in 2023 used applicant

tracking systems (ATS) for hiring employees[14]. ATS is used to track those who are applying for positions at a company. The important thing for a job seeker to know about ATS is that the system will generally parse resumes for keywords that relate to the job position.

A strategy to help you better your odds of an interview would be for you to validate that pertinent keywords listed in the job posting are also on your resume. For example, a job posting lists that the applicant should have a general understanding of how Microsoft PowerPoint works. If you're an applicant who fits that criteria ensure you have it listed on your resume.

Recruiters on average spend only 7.4 seconds parsing through a resume at first glance[15]. You need to make sure that at first glance the recruiter gains interest within those first six to seven seconds. I would highly recommend that you visit your local high school/college's career center to get your resume reviewed. Especially if this is your first time creating one. Have a few professional eyes look at it for accuracy.

Characteristics of a Good Resume:

- Formatting: your resume should be formatted without any errors. Spacing should be the same throughout. As someone who's interviewed hundreds of applicants I can tell you that if spacing is off or there are spelling mistakes you better have a stellar interview if you want the job. If you can't take the time to get your own resume in the right format, how can I expect you to perform the same way for my clients? Perception is reality and grammar errors are no bueno.

- Relevant work history: Use present tense when describing attributes for your current position and past tense to describe past job positions. When applying for your first job position after college it may be wise to include part time jobs, but after a few years of corporate experience it may be wise to drop off that part time job at the jewelry store you did in college. You deserve credit for the job, but it's not as relevant to the job you're seeking anymore at that point and may distract the recruiter from more important parts of your resume. Include past jobs that relate to your current role and to those which skills will translate to the potential new role.
- Educational background: ensure you're listing out your high school or full college degree and when graduation is planned. You should honestly exclude your GPA if it's average or below average.
- Top of resume: Have your name listed up top with a bigger text size than the rest of your resume. Think about bolding your name as well if it fits the format. You don't need to have your full home address listed on your resume—the city and state will work just fine. Especially if you post your resume on a job site and it gets floated around like Taylor Swift's next album. Personally, I

wouldn't want to give someone my full address unless they're interviewing me or I'm applying on their company website.

- Email address should be professional: do not use your weird email from middle school flybirdiefly@gmail.com or junglefever123@gmail.com. This should be common sense, but I've interviewed many interns with weirder email addresses. Gmail is a free service you can use to create an email address with your name simply listed. For example, ali.qasim@gmail.com or aliqasim@gmail.com. If the name is not available then add numbers, but no adjectives please. Add your LinkedIn link to the top of your resume and make it a link to be clicked. If you're on google docs you would first need to paste the full link onto your resume. Highlight the link and select 'insert link'. Have the text on your resume say 'LinkedIn', but when the link is clicked it should take the reader to your actual LinkedIn page.
- PDF: I would strongly recommend that you create a version of your resume in PDF once you're done reviewing your resume in Microsoft Word or Google Docs. Both programs have the option for free for you to create a PDF version of your resume. This locks your resume from editing and creates a more professional look for the reader. Review the PDF after you create the new version and send out the PDF version to prospective employers.
- Take the time to do mock interviews with mentors or colleagues and point blank ask the reviewer for constructive criticism. You

don't want the friend who's just going to say you did a great job—that's the easy way out. There's generally always room for improvement (especially straight out of college). Pobody's nerfect (a reference to The Good Place—IYKYK). You must expect perfection for yourself but understand that perfection is never achievable. Getting as close to it as possible is the goal.

Another tactic to give yourself a leg up on the competition is to look through your entire LinkedIn network and find colleagues that work at a company with a job opening in which you have interest. Message them on LinkedIn and ask them if they're well. Then say that you're interested in a role at the company and want to learn more about the culture of the organization and how they operate as you're going to apply for roles soon. Near the end of the discussion ask them if they think you'd be a good fit for the role and if they'd be willing to refer you. Many times they'll say yes. This can happen over online chat or over the phone. The phone is usually more effective, but chat can also work in this situation. Remember they may be incentivized via referral bonus to refer you, but it won't be a cakewalk. They want to make sure you represent them well as they're currently employed at the company in which you're potentially be interviewing.

Word of advice during your conversation: ask these contacts how the referral process works before you apply for the role online. At many organizations internal employees have to refer you on an internal system for a role before you formally apply for the role in order for the referral to count. Recruiters in HR love referrals and they're more likely to take more than 6-7 seconds to actually read through your resume and schedule an initial recruiter screen if you're referred.

During the interview process don't forget to send thank you emails after every interview to the recruiters and those who interviewed you whether you get the job or not. My colleagues and I have had plenty of occasions where recruiters reached back out to us even when we didn't get the job for another position. Keep a good relationship with recruiters and it may come handy someday.

The Offer and Negotiation

When you receive an offer the first thing to do is be humble and thank the recruiter or hiring manager for the offer. Next, ask them if the offer is open for negotiation. Always try to negotiate and see what else they can offer. Recruiters will always be cordial and make it seem like they're on your side. This is a cardinal sin to believe… and it's complete **BS**. HR will generally look out for the organization before the employee no matter what they tell you. It's quite literally in their job description. Recruiters will generally try to get you in at the lowest part of the 'range' possible because their performance is based on those metrics and more.

Always ask for $5,000-$10,000 more than what you really want so if they negotiate down you may still be close to the figure you were looking for. This truly depends on how much leverage and experience you have. The recruiter could ask for a salary range that would peak your interest. Don't fall for the trap. Ask them what the salary range is for the position. They may not disclose the range. If they force you to tell them a range, tell them within $5,000-$10,000 of what you actually want. For example, if you'd be fine with a $60,000 base salary for the role, tell them $65,000 base or $60,000-$65,000 base. Always give yourself a cushion in case they come with a lower number. This can happen in the first interview or during the offer process. Either way, unless they're off by $20,000 more or less, keep interviewing and try to convince them you're worth it. If they fall in love with you as a candidate it's always possible they find the money.

6

THRIVING AT YOUR NEW ROLE

You got the job! Well done. Seriously give yourself a pat on the back for the achievement. Getting to this point is not easy and can be mentally draining for many on the job hunt.

Seven Tips for Success in Your New Role

1. Industry term: be a sponge—take notes during orientation and when you meet your manager for the first few weeks. Write

down the organizational acronyms and any notes pertaining to your job responsibilities as you'll need to know them.

2. Dress in business professional for your first day. It shows how serious you are for the role. After a few days, get a vibe for how everyone else dresses and go from there. Over time it's advised to shift to the duck theory to improve your odds of promotion which is described in a previous chapter.

3. Be active and attend company events with a smile. Get a little personal with your colleagues and management so they'll remember you better. And I mean a little… there's a difference between talking about your family and boasting about how you got super lit in college. Avoid politics and other sensitive topics until you truly get to know someone as a friend in the organization. It's not worth the risk of offending someone in management or someone you may be working closely with one day. Keep to a two-drink maximum until you get to know people better and gain trust with certain folks.

4. Learn how to speak like your colleagues. Management will likely be 10-20 years older than you and if you talk about how you 'got lit' last weekend, 'did it for the plot', 'avoided simps', and 'slayed' they're probably going to look at you like you're crazy and laugh it off, but ultimately you will seem unprofessional. These first impressions are paramount to your success, and you

don't want to seem like you're not fitting their vibe. One day when you're in management you can have your employees 'fit your vibe'. Until then they have the power, and you should follow their lead.

5. Try your best to not form romantic relationships with your colleagues. Unless you're confident you both will fall in love and form a long-term relationship, steer clear of your co-workers. If things don't work out it can come back to bite you hard and cause your ex's close co-workers to potentially dislike you.

6. Learn the system. I could honestly write a whole chapter on this, but I'll keep it short. If you want to increase likelihood of success and promotion you need to learn how the game is played. You need to learn more about the system and work environment you're a part of so you can take advantage of every rule possible at the appropriate time to give you an advantage. These advantages can help you potentially perform better than your colleagues and put you in better positions for raises and promotions. You need to figure out what you can and can't do within the system so you can make better decisions and ultimately perform better. You also need to know where there are gray areas.

   Gray areas are situations where it's difficult to know what the rules are because they're not firmly set for a use case. For example, while in college I used to work part-time in at a department clothing store. I am partially color-blind so giving people advice on clothes was an interesting challenge for me. They didn't ask me if I was color-blind so I never had an opportunity to disclose. We would get an employee discount of 30% off any clothes we wanted in the store and also 30% off gift cards. Normally co-workers would buy the gift cards using the discount for family members as gifts. After learning about the rules I wondered – what would stop an employee from buying a gift card at 30% off and then going to a different express, getting the employee discount at 30% and then paying with the 30% off gift card. It would be like getting 30% off twice for each transaction. I read the handbook – there were no rules specifically stating I couldn't do this. I tried it for myself and was successful. This would be an example of a loophole/gray area – it's probably something they shouldn't allow, but it's not directly stated that it's not allowed in the rules. Before operating in gray areas though I would recommend you learn everything you can about the system you're a part of before you start looking into gray areas/loopholes in the system. It's not worth losing your job over.

7. This last tip may seem a little harsh, but you'll learn over time that nobody in the professional world truly cares about what college you went to or that you were the president of some club. You may be able to start a conversation with those variables, but

it can only help you so much. Your college experience is what helped you get your foot in the door and landed you the job. When you start a new job you're truly starting over on a new slate just like you did when you started college. What your new organization will likely care about more is your performance and the relationship you're building with management and your colleagues.

At the end of the day, you gotta put your head down and do the work. Keep up the professional development and don't be okay with staying stagnant. Continue learning about your industry and from those who operate your position at a high level. Obtain certifications. Find ways to bring more value to your organization. If your employers don't recognize your efforts with promotions or raises I promise you'll be able to find a new employer who will. You'll also find that just being book smart is not necessarily conducive to gaining promotions. Find ways to be street smart as well; build relationships and create new value for the organization. Sadly, popularity and perception does matter within organizations. Keep a good reputation with everyone at work (even the janitor) and be nice to management.

After a Few Years on the Job…

Take a look around the job market and see what else is out there. Organizations love hiring newbies fresh from college because they're cheap talent. They can overwork you for a variety of reasons and because you're young, new and wanting to learn they'll likely take advantage of the situation. I'm sure your manager/employer cares about you to an extent. They'll walk the walk, but if they have to choose between a higher profit margin and laying you off they're going to do the latter.

I would highly recommend investigating a jump to a different company using the connections you built up. After two-to-three years of experience, if you're not satisfied with your pay and experience at your current organization, update your resume and start looking around for a role that pays better. You always want to be paid what the market dictates, not what an organization says they can afford. Some organizations reward high performers with good raises, but some do not and make the excuse that they 'don't have the budget'. That is generally **BS**. It's important to stretch your interview muscle every now and then to ensure you're up to the task if you have an impromptu interview. Take some interviews and see if you get any offers. Then it's your decision and you have the power to make it. Go get your bag—no one else will get it for you.

Another benefit to looking for a new employer after a few years of working is that you'll have a better understanding of what you're looking for in an employer contrary to how you felt when you were first looking for a job. You'll also have an opportunity to start fresh with a new organization and develop new connections.

Caveat: it's always possible that the organization that you're working for is paying you well and promoting you without you having to jump ship. That means they truly like you/your work and they see a future for you within the organization. This is a great sight and something we hope to see from more organizations in the future.

7

FINANCIAL SUCCESS

Why go to college and get a job? Is it because you're passionate about your job or you enjoy kumbaya with your co-workers around the water cooler? It's MONEY. Anyone telling you otherwise is **PARTIALLY BSing** you. There are other factors of reason to take this journey, but the main attraction is you likely want financial success for a variety of reasons. Some reason could include a better life for your family, starting your own family, dreams of entrepreneurship and the ambition of traveling the world. No matter what your reason you need a good income to pursue it without putting yourself in bad situations for the long-term.

There's no quick, get rich scheme or trick I can give you to turn you magically into a millionaire in the coming years. If anyone tries to sell you a course on that topic I would avoid it at all costs. Think about it: if they're making so much money with their strategy why would they sell it to you for peanuts? Why increase their competition? They'll likely say it's because they want to help others, but I call **BS**. If they want to help others they can donate to a nonprofit or sell you the course free of charge. It's always about the money and we can't let naivete set us back. When they start selling courses it generally means there's too much competition for them in that space and they want to capitalize on the hype while they can by selling you their now broken business model. 99% of the time it's **BS** – don't fall for that trap.

Retirement Benefits

A key component to your pay is actually what benefits an organization offers. Base salary and bonus are important, but if the organization does not have benefits you might have to pay for those yourself.

Retirement is important because it's your gateway to finish your working career. For those working your normal 40 hours a week job you're giving up your time for money. At some point though don't you want your time to be spent doing what's you truly want? If you make the right decisions earlier in your career you might also have the option to end your career early as well. And we like options don't we? Options to pursue your passion, spend more time with family or take a month long vacation in Europe?

You may also be thinking 'I'm in my 20s. Why do I need to think about retirement? That's SO FAR AWAY!'

Yes it is SO FAR AWAY and that's exactly why you need to start sooner rather than later. The longer you can let your investments sit in a good index fund the longer it has to grow. And the sooner you'll have the option for retirement. An index fund is a fund that includes investment in generally hundreds of company stock within a fund.

Since there are hundreds of companies within the index if one company in the fund drops in price the whole fund is less likely to fall as much as that one company did. Compound interest is your best friend here. Time in the market is more important than timing the market. You need to start investing as early as possible and as much as possible in your 20s. Let me break down why that should be the case. I'm about to make you a lot of money for your retirement.

The disclaimer below is to project myself legally as the following could be perceived to be financial advice:

Disclaimer: The material herein is provided for informational purposes only and should not be construed as investment advice or an offer or solicitation to buy or sell securities. The material is not intended to be used as a general guide to investing, or as a source of any specific investment recommendations, and makes no implied or express recommendations concerning the manner in which any client's account should or would be handled, as appropriate investment strategies depend upon the client's investment objectives.

I discuss the S&P 500 index fund quite a bit in the pages that follow. S&P stands for Standard and Poors and the 500 represents 500 best performing publicly traded companies at the current time[16]. It represents a diverse selection of top U.S. companies; some companies may be replaced every quarter if they're not performing up to standard. I have no clue why it's called Standard and Poor, but it was first launched in 1923. From 1957 to 2023 it has given investors an average return of 10.23% annual return on average. From 2003 to 2023 the annual return was very similar at 10.2% on average[18]. I don't mean to bore you with numbers, but what I'm trying to get at is this fund is one of the most consistently performing funds on the market and it's been that way for decades.

The financial exercise below shows exactly why you should start investing in your retirement in your 20s instead of your 30s. Assumptions below are listed to give you more clarity on the controls of the exercise.

Assumptions:

- You gain 7% return annually on your investments. For example, if you put $100 into a fund in January 2023 by January 2024 the investment should theoretically be worth $107. That would be a 7% annual return on investment. This is lower than average S&P 500's past returns as indicated in previous pages.
- Assumption is at $80,000 salary your entire career and you retire at 65. For the purposes of this exercise I kept salary stagnant. For most their salary continues to rise slowly throughout their career.

Retirement Exercise[17]

Starting Age	Contribution %	Salary	Employer Match	Your Total Contributions	Estimated Retirement Fund
22	6%	$80,000	0%	$206,400	**$1,189,327.18**
32	6%	$80,000	0%	$158,400	**$570,880.44**
22	6%	$80,000	3%	$206,400	**$1,783,990.77**
32	6%	$80,000	3%	$158,400	**$856,320.66**

Takeaways:

- There is a difference of $618,446.74 if you started at 32 instead of 22 with your difference in contributions of only $48,000. If you include the 401k employer match the difference balloons to $927,670.11 with the same difference in contributions. That is the power of time in the market – the earlier you start the more time your money has to organically grow via investment gains.
- If you start investing in your retirement at 32 instead of 22 **it can cost you hundreds of thousands of dollars** of potential gains whether you have the employer match or not. Start investing in your retirement as early as possible.

You may be thinking why do I need so much money in retirement? Well young buck as you make more money over your career you'll probably start spending more of your income on yourself and your family. When you decide to retire you'll need money to hold you over and you'll probably want to maintain a certain lifestyle in your remaining years. Medical technology is also continuously advancing keeping the average person alive for longer. Longer life means more money will be needed in retirement to sustain your lifestyle. I wouldn't depend on social security or the government for your retirement. If you start in your 40s and find out you need millions in your fund for retirement to sustain your lifestyle you'll likely be paying <u>thousands a month</u> to catch up instead of hundreds. Start investing in your retirement earlier rather than later.

Quick Tip: You're generally able to borrow from your retirement accounts for expenses, emergencies or even buying your first home. I would recommend to avoid borrowing from these accounts unless you have an emergency.

The next part of the equation is your investment strategy. Just because you put your money in a 401k or Roth 401k retirement account doesn't mean it's being invested in the right place. You actually have to invest your dollars into a fund. When you start working for an employer who offers a 401k option you may get enrolled into a target date fund automatically. Being enrolled in a target date fund is better than being enrolled in nothing, but I'll explain why it may not be the best fit in the coming pages.

Talking to a financial advisor is a good use of your time—but don't pay for one. Most financial advisors don't beat the S&P 500 annually. They may tell you to put money into a target date fund or diversify into some random investments that did well in the previous years. This is **absolute BS** and I say that with a passion.

The dirty little secret is that financial advisors likely won't tell you to just put your money in S&P 500 and let it sit there. That's because at that point you won't need them anymore. Don't pay financial advisors to give you a smaller return on investment.

Target date funds will have bonds and other funds that don't give much as much of a return. From 1988 to 2023 the average bond return was 6.1% annually[20]. This is a lower return than the S&P 500 fund I was mentioning above. I would advise to not have more than 10% of your retirement portfolio to include bond investments. A portfolio is a collection of assets. In this case for a retirement fund it would be stocks, bonds, cash, or mutual funds.

This is because while you're young you need growth to build a large portfolio. I would advise investing in a simple S&P 500 fund and letting it sit there over time. You don't need to wait for a dip in the market – just invest in it slowly over the long term. Fidelity has this fund as FXAIX and Vanguard as VOO. It's standard practice for most 401k issuers to have the S&P 500 as an investment fund of choice. You can always move those funds to target date funds or bonds in your 50s once you build a large nest egg. Some years the fund may lose 3-5% and some years it may gain 20%. Returns are not set in stone and will change every year. Let it sit there and grow; don't look at it daily or you'll drive yourself crazy. Focus on your day job and improving your salary over time. I would not advise day trading or swing trading unless it's going to be a full time job. There is just as much knowledge to learn as your day-job about the market to even make a solid attempt at being successful. It's much more lucrative to focus on moving up at your company then trying to trade your way to a larger account balance.

In summary, from the ages of 20 to around 50 you should invest most of your retirement contributions into a simple S&P 500 fund and let it grow during those time periods. After 50 start thinking about diversifying your fund into safer investments if your fund has enough to sustain you in retirement. Maybe at that point it would be time to talk to that financial advisor, but again don't pay for one. The brokerage you're using for your retirement portfolio may have financial advisors to help you for free. Talk to mentors or people in your trusted circle for advice. Do your own research.

Business tycoon Warren Buffett famously made a million-dollar bet with a hedge fund in 2008 that his simple investment in Vanguard's S&P 500 Admiral fund would outpace the hedge fund's investment portfolio over the next 10 years (Anyone can invest in this fund or a similar S&P 500 fund—just make an account with Vanguard or any brokerage and you're all set). Hedge funds are corporations with employees whose sole purpose is to get the best return on investment for their investors. Buffett's simple S&P 500 strategy gave him a return of 7.1% annually during that time period. The hedge fund after their fees gave a return of 2.2% annually to their investors[19]. If a high-priced hedge fund that trades and watches the market daily like a hawk can't beat the S&P 500 why do you believe you can?

Most good S&P 500 funds give great returns with a low expense ratio. The expense ratio is what it costs to run the fund. Some fancy funds have expense ratios of 0.5% to 1% annually. That may not seem like a lot at first but can add up to tens of thousands of dollars by the time you retire and most of those funds don't beat the S&P 500 either in the long run.

I would also strongly advise to not trade individual stocks too much either unless it's going to be your full-time job. Focus on your day job and professional development. Your increases in salary by focusing on your day job over time will give you more financial flexibility to increase contributions in retirement.

You'll likely get the option to invest in a pre-tax 401k or possibly a post-tax Roth 401k through your employer. The pre-tax 401k means your contributions to the 401k come out of your paycheck before taxes, but you pay those taxes when you pull out dollars during retirement. The post-tax means your contributions to your Roth 401k come out of your paycheck after taxes, but at retirement age pulling money out of the fund is tax free. Basically you pay taxes on your investments now or pay them at retirement.

Not all employers offer the post-tax Roth 401k. There have been thousands of studies on this, and—honestly—I don't see a considerable difference between investing in the pre-tax fund vs post-tax fund. Based on your situation you may be in a lower tax bracket when you retire, therefore, if you pull out cash from your 401k you'll be paying less in taxes. The opposite could also be true. I personally have both Roth and 401k dollars in my retirement account and when the market has a considerable dip I call up my brokerage (Fidelity) to convert my 401k dollars to a Roth. I do this when the market dips so that I have to pay less in taxes to convert the 401k to Roth. This is an **advanced strategy** therefore do your own research and ask colleagues or mentors what they do for retirement as well.

Health Insurance

Healthcare can be expensive. If you're relatively healthy in your 20s choose the highest deductible healthcare plan (which is generally the cheapest) and consider contributing to a health savings account (HSA). An HSA is exactly what it sounds like—a savings account for future healthcare expenses. If your company matches your HSA contribution then I would highly recommend for you to contribute to an HSA. If you're relatively healthy and don't expect any big healthcare expenses you don't need to be paying high premiums for expensive healthcare plans that you'll never fully use.

Bet on yourself.

Save the dollars you'd spend on a higher priced healthcare plan and invest it into your retirement, HSA account or your emergency fund. If you want to do the math check the annual cost of premiums on the highest deductible plan vs the lower deductible plans you're considering. Let's say the difference is $3,000. Do you plan to spend $3,000 on healthcare expenses for the year? If the answer is 'no' then it's better that you keep the $3,000 in your pocket or invest it instead of permanently handing it over to the insurance company. It's always better for YOU to have control over your money than handing it over to someone else. There's no refunds when you pay insurance premiums.

Generally high deductible health plans allow you to contribute to an HSA. The HSA is a very powerful tool for growing your wealth and health over time. This is not to be confused with an FSA plan in which the dollars have to be used within a certain amount of time. HSA contributions are triple tax advantaged and never expire. They're contributed pre-tax (reducing your taxable income), withdrawals for medical expenses are tax free, and investment gains on HSA dollars are tax free.

Healthcare is very expensive in the U.S., and I can promise you you'll end up using this account many times for healthcare expenses—especially if you end up having kids. You can also use the dollars for cosmetic work. For example, I used HSA dollars to get laser eye surgery a few years ago. I paid for half with savings I accumulated in my HSA and the other half with my credit card. I was able to reimburse myself the $2,000 I paid with my credit card (we love our points) over time, from my HSA account with my tax-free contributions. If you plan to do this someday keep your receipts. After you attain more than $1,000 in your HSA account you can generally invest the dollars above $1,000 into index funds.

Dental Insurance

Dental plans are important. Sign up and get your teeth cleaned twice a year (generally included with your dental plan). Dental expenses can stack up fast if you don't take care of your teeth. I just realized I'm starting to sound like my mother…

Life Insurance

The final topic I want to cover here is life insurance. My parents are big fans of life insurance. Back in the day I could understand wanting to leave something for your loved ones 'in case something was to happen'. Times have changed. In their day they did not have the liberty to go online freely, make an account and invest in the market ourselves like we can. Today you can invest in safe index funds, and they could be worth millions of dollars over decades of time.

For example, let's say someone invested $900 a month for a $1 million-dollar whole life insurance policy over a 50-year period. That's $540,000 in contributions for a $1 million dollar return at death for your beneficiaries. You'd make $460,000 on that investment. That sounds nice, but there's a big opportunity cost of making that investment. Instead, if you take that $900 a month and invest in a fund like the S&P 500 over 50 years with a 7% annual return (which is conservative) you'd have $4,555,265.37[17]. An opportunity cost is the value of an alternative that was not taken. In this scenario - the math ain't mathin. This is exactly what the life insurance company is doing with your $900 a month premium. They're investing the money they receive from you and keeping the difference between the payout and gains on investing your dollars. Opting for the life insurance route vs just investing the premiums into S&P 500 would've had an opportunity cost of over 3.5 million dollars.

Do your own research, but I would recommend cutting out the middleman and investing the money yourself. You may be thinking 'what if I die early and don't have anything for my family?'

Nowadays you can get a term life policy worth hundreds of thousands of dollars for fewer than $100 a month as long as you're young and healthy. Have the length of the life insurance term cover your family until retirement. Before retirement age you'll have that term life policy, and at retirement you'll have your 401k/IRA retirement fund to cover your family in case of death. You'll be in a much better financial position if you operate with this strategy. Your company may also offer life insurance benefits as well that covers you based on your salary at time of death or offer plans that are priced well compared to the market.

FIRE

There are many paths to becoming financially successful and achieving financial independence. Financial independence theoretically would allow you to quit your job and allow you to pursue what truly makes you happy. Possibly pursuing your actual passion or spending more time with family. Many concepts here are similar to the financial independence retire early (FIRE) movement that is raging on Reddit forums. The goal is for people to amass wealth earlier in their lives so they can retire in their 50s, 40s, or even 30s.

A structured strategy will need to be in place so you can achieve this goal if it's something you'd like to do. If it's not something you'd like to take on all at once, maybe work towards bits and pieces of the strategy so you can build better financial habits and health for you and your family. Again, these are **aggressive**, but calculated strategies to help you potentially retire early. Even if that doesn't apply to you I would still advise to read through this section as you may be in a position to take this approach someday.

If you do a quick google search this can get much more technical and granular, but here's my version of FIRE.

Step 1: Building Your Emergency Fund

The first step to financial security is to build a three-to-six-month fund for emergency expenses. Emergency expenses could include your car breaking down, home repairs, unexpected hospital bills and more. Honestly whether you're going for FIRE or not you should always have an emergency fund. Being forced to sign up for high interest loans when you have a financial emergency will set you back financially. If you ever use any funds from the account for an emergency, replenish it at the next opportunity. To calculate how much you'd need in that fund simply take a monthly average of all your expenses and multiply it by the number of months in which you would want the fund to include.

I would advise to put the emergency funds in a high yield savings account so it can grow risk free as well and is easily accessible. The big brick and mortar banks like Chase, Bank of America, Wells Fargo, and more provide savings accounts, but the return is absolute garbage—as little as 0.01% return on investment annually[21]. Just like the life insurance companies they're taking your savings and investing it themselves to keep the difference.

Do a Google search for high yield savings accounts and you'll find numerous safe and Federal Deposit Insurance Corporation (FDIC) insured banks that provide 1% return annual percentage yield (APY) at the minimum. In writing this book as of July 2024 you can easily get 3-4% annual return for money that you would've had sitting in a bank account anyways. Many of these are online banks so please do your research on them before making the jump. You should try to find a credible bank that provides the best return. Research to find the best return: 1% doesn't sound like much, but at least you're earning something for keeping your cash with their bank. Banks take your hard-earned money and loan it out to consumers and businesses for massive returns. You deserve a portion of those returns as well.

Step 2: Methods to FIRE

Plan A: Maximize your 401k/Roth

Max out your 401k or Roth IRA accounts annually to the limit. Work for a company that has a great match and you're off to the races. The earlier you start maxing out your retirement accounts the sooner you'll have the opportunity to retire early. I outlined what funds to invest in earlier in the chapter and the opportunity cost for waiting too long to start investing in your retirement—feel free to reference if needed.

As of Q4 2023 the median 401k balance for people in their 20s was $6,100; 30s was $20,500; and 40s was $38,600[24]. In my opinion, these are horrible numbers whether you're going for FIRE or not. You need to fund your retirement accounts early and aggressively if you truly want to retire early or even retire on time.

Plan B. 401k Contributions up to the Match and Invest in Real Estate

Another method is to make 401k contributions up to your company's match and take the remaining funds to purchase real estate investment properties. For example, if your company matches 50% of your 401k contributions up to 6% you would contribute only up to 6% so your company would match their 3%. You should ALWAYS take the company match at the minimum – it's essentially free money as long as you're making your contributions.

Next, you would save for a down payment on a home that would eventually become an investment property. You could buy the home and live in it until you save enough to buy another home. Buy the next home (also a potential investment property) and turn your existing primary home into an investment property.

Aim to buy another property every two-to-five years (depending on how much you can save) and turn the existing property into an investment home. Depending on your situation you can also buy investment properties and turn them immediately into investment homes instead of living in them first. Moving is a drag—I know. The combination of the retirement account and the investment properties is a diversified play on FIRE. You'll have plenty of time to refinance the investment property mortgages if needed to build a consistent source of income while renting the property out. Don't overpay for the investment home – wait for the right deal. During retirement you'll have social security, real estate investment income, and your 401k retirement fund to hold you over.

Plan C. RSUs Combined with Methods A and/or B

The third method is a potential add on onto the first two methods. Or you could pick one or two of the methods A or B; or even strive for all three methods if this is possible for you. This method is for those who are willing to take more risk or sell their soul (figuratively) to corporations.

You would need to earn an opportunity to gain restricted stock units (RSUs) for staying employed with a company and help the company grow their revenues and stock price over time. When you have enough shares of stock in the company you can sell the stock and live off of the proceeds.

For example, in higher level positions with early-stage or large corporations they may offer 40,000 shares of stock in the company if you work with the company for four years. If you leave before the four-year term you could receive part of the 40,000 shares or nothing at all depending on how the deal is structured. This approach is not available at your everyday job and probably not available to those right out of college. You'd need to get experience and leverage your learnings to gain a high-level position at a company or a position that a company desperately needs. Otherwise, you'd need to start your own company, build up the value of the company and either live off the profits or sell.

These methods sound fine and dandy, but how do you come up with the income to max out your 401k and pay for normal necessities? The first part is having a high paying job. Following the earlier parts of this book on choosing a major and the right job will guide you on that path. Next, you will need to live below your means and cut down on expenditures.

Sacrificing for Wealth Creation

In this day and age, we need to redefine what who we believe to be rich or wealthy. There are millions of people out there who have fancy cars, clothes, and homes—but can they truly afford them? Are they truly at that level of wealth in which they can take on all of those expenses and not live month to month? It's very probable these folks are living above their means trying to 'fake it until they make it'. What they're trying to make honestly beats me. This is a form of **BS** in which most people who are living those fancy lifestyles are trying to sell with their "status" or ego.

Become friends with a bank teller and you'll hear that those with the largest accounts do not generally drive Range Rovers and wear Louis Vuitton gear. There are some that do, but more often than not the wealthy drive a Lexus or Toyota. A Honda or an Acura. They also don't walk into the bank Gucci'd to the toes. They live below their means and invest their money over long stretches of time. Splurge every now and then, but only if they're ahead of their financial goals.

Per financial guru Dave Ramsey, "Very few people who look like they have money actually do… The huge car, expensive car, the vastly expensive vacation on Instagram, the vastly expensive fill-in-the-blank, are very seldom actual indicators of wealth" [27].

Fancy fancy fancy is expensive expensive expensive. Drake famously released a song called Fancy in which the chorus goes "Oh you fancy huh? Nails done hair done everything did". Our version of this is "Oh you fiscally responsible huh? Emergency fund done, 401k done, we all fiscally did".

A survey completed by LendingTree showed that 51% of Gen Z respondents feel financial pressure to keep up with someone within their circle, such as a family member or friend. The survey also found that 51% admitted to overspending to impress others and 56% were in debt because of the overspending[27].

Honest Tip: just because something is on sale is NOT a reason to make a purchase. If you don't need it, don't buy it. A discount of 50% off a $100 coat could make it $50, but you're still spending $50. If you don't buy it you spend nothing. Choose nothing more often. Honestly, I've tried to teach my wife this concept and failed miserably.... Love always prevails.

You need to care less about what your friends think about you. As soon as you try to keep up with the Joneses you've already lost. If you care what people say you'll be stuck in the same loop with them. If you don't have the disposable income to keep up with the Joneses don't keep up with them. Swallow your pride and let it go.

Living below your means can be defined as having a set budget for yourself month-to-month and following it. Keep it simple.

Here's a common budgeting breakdown you should try to stick to:

- 30% of your income to rent or a mortgage;
- 20% of your income towards transportation, utilities, and insurance;
- 20% of your income towards food, clothes, and living expenses that can vary month-to-month;
- 10% of your income towards savings and investments; and
- 10% towards your emergency fund.

After your emergency fund is built, put the remaining 10% towards vacations or splurging on yourself. You earned the money! You deserve to spend on yourself but do it responsibly. Build up your emergency fund first and then splurge sensibly.

If you can put more income towards savings or investments that is AWESOME. Another method to lower rent expenses is to live with multiple roommates. Sacrifice and you'll be well rewarded over time.

Another popular method this century is being a DINK. If you remember from earlier, DINK stands for double income no kids. Moving in with your significant other/spouse and combining your incomes while you do not have kids is a great way to build wealth. You and your spouse should have a decent amount of discretionary or 'disposable' income after you pay all of your bills if you both have good incomes. Although you may have more income, stick to the plan and don't live month-to-month. You still need to live below your means. Don't forget weddings, diamond rings, homes and kids are expensive – you need save for big life events. Living with your parents is also another avenue to cutting down on rent expenses and increasing your discretionary income.

Minimizing Distractions

In previous generations people would go take a walk if they were bored, explore the great outdoors or say hi to their neighbors. Nowadays the internet is so advanced that we can simply turn on Netflix at any time or look at social media at our leisure. The innovation is immaculate, but a problem arises when we spend too much time on these distractions instead of focusing on family or our goals.

Think about it this way: every time you use social media or watch Netflix you're actually making money for the company that owns that platform. It may be free for you to use, but the company is making money from your data, your subscription and by showing you ads. Believe me it's addictive. We all enjoy it. My parents used to get mad at me for using my phone so much, but after I taught them how to use it they became addicted themselves. There's nothing wrong with using social media and watching TV, but try to keep it to a minimum. If it helps you relax—great—but, at a certain point, continue your focus on your career and family as well.

Helping Others

Picture this scenario: you have a good job and you've started putting some income in a savings account. Things are going well, and you've saved about $20,000 in a high-yield savings account as your emergency fund. You start splurging on yourself a little and you're following strategies listed in this book. Others notice and start to inquire about your newfound success.

Your cousin, Doug, notices your success and starts to talk to you more than he normally does. You went to high school with Doug and always felt bad for him. Luck never really went his way and he always had problems with relationships and money. He works part-time at the local Home Depot as a cashier. He comes to you and asks for a $5,000 loan to resolve a gambling debt. Do you help him?

This is where things get tricky. You feel bad for him and he's family. You truly want to help him, but gambling is a tricky situation and it's potentially giving an addict more money to fuel his addiction. Let's be real—you need to think about this situation rationally and without emotion. You should NOT give him the full $5,000. Here's why:

- He may be family, but he works a part time job and likely doesn't have the capability to pay you back anytime soon.
- Money is one of the biggest reasons why relationships between family and spouses fail. If he can't pay you back it'll cause a rift in your relationship with Doug and awkwardness every Thanksgiving. It's also a hassle trying to recover your loan from him as well.
- You don't owe Doug jack shit. At the end of the day, you made the right decisions in life to get you to this point. Doug didn't make the right decisions and should bear the consequences. Him bearing the consequences will teach him why he should not excessively gamble in the first place with money he doesn't have.

- Doug barely talks to you—you don't think he's already asked the people he actually talks to on the daily already for money? If he's asking you that means they already said no and there's probably a reason for that… don't be naïve.

The right answer would be to give him no money. If you truly want to help him you want to make sure he doesn't fall into the situation again. You want to help him curb his gambling addiction. I know you may feel like a snitch but get his immediate family members involved and ask them to help with the situation.

If you still feel like you should help him in some capacity then give him $500 to $1,000 but do it the way magnate Kevin O'Leary loans his family money. He tells them he will give them the money, but this is the only time in their lifetime he will help them. They cannot ask for money again—especially if they don't pay you back. You have to make that VERY CLEAR. Then it's up to Doug on whether he's really that desperate for the cash or he wants to save his ask for another day.

Credit Cards

You'll realize over the years that most people have different opinions on credit cards. Your parents, best friends and your spouse may all have different feelings on the matter. Some people avoid them like the plague, some use them only for emergencies, and some swipe like they'll never have to pay it back. Credit cards can be dangerous, but can also be very useful depending on how they're utilized. As we discussed in the last chapter – you need to learn the system.

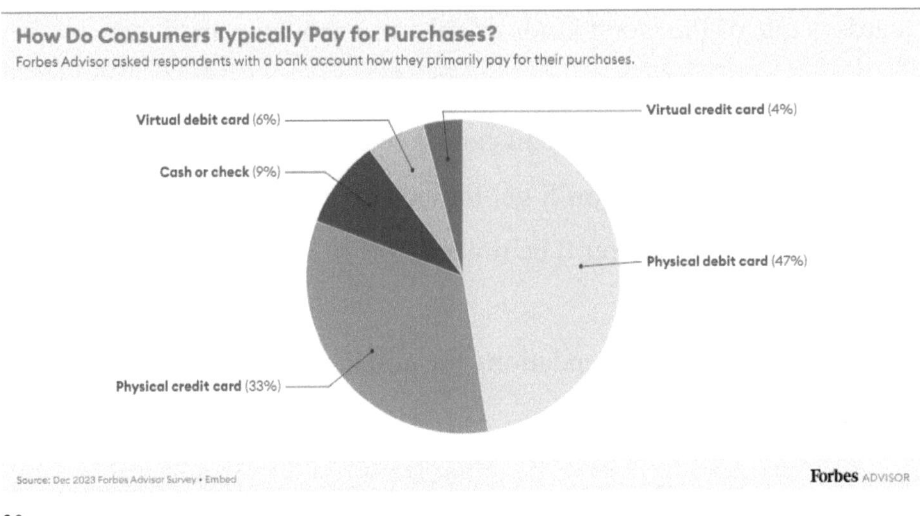

30

Over 37% of survey respondents in the Forbes Survey above used a virtual or physical credit card for purchases. Physical debit cards made up the majority at 47%[30].

Personally, I always use credit cards as my first choice for every transaction. I only use my debit card if the merchant does not accept credit cards for the transaction.

Famous financial guru Dave Ramsey tells his followers to avoid credit cards whatsoever. He famously carries around a large pair of scissors at events to cut up credit cards. One of his key reasons is that "responsible use of credit cards doesn't exist"[29]. He's partially correct on his assessment. The people that need his company's advice on finances generally have lots of credit card debt.

If you cannot control the spending on your credit card you will eventually rack up too much credit card debt. Debt from credit cards is one of the worst kinds of debt you can have and it can definitely set you back for years trying to recover back to good financial health. Using a credit card is like playing with fire – if you don't follow the rules you'll get buried (with debt of course). Follow these guidelines and you'll be rewarded.

Here are seven recommendations for utilizing credit cards responsibly:

1. Always pay the full statement balance when it's due.

In the paragraphs above I discussed using credit cards "responsibly". One part of the responsibility is that you should always pay the full balance on your statement every single month. Credit card companies will give you the option to make a "minimum payment" and it will be a much more appealing dollar figure compared to the statement balance that's due in full. The minimum payment is **BS.** If you only make the minimum payment the next month the remainder of the statement balance from the previous month will still be due PLUS INTEREST. We do not like paying interest. We like earning interest.

Keep only making minimum payments over time and the interest due will continue to increase and compound against you. As of July 2024 the median credit card interest rate is 24.72%[31]. Meaning if you had $1,000 remaining on your statement balance with that interest rate you would be paying $20.52 in interest on top of that previous statement balance. Doesn't sound like much, but if not paid in full the next month's interest will include the previous month's interest. This can compound quickly and soon enough your interest payments will overtake the principal balance you had the first place. If you do not have a steady income to manage the debt responsibly, you should not get a credit card in the first place or only have a credit card for emergencies.

Paying interest on a credit card is a cardinal sin. Anyone telling you otherwise is full of **BS**. Don't ever put yourself in a position in which you cannot pay the full statement balance on your credit card. I have never paid interest to a credit card company and I never will. That's not because I'm "wealthy". It's because I'm responsible with my money. I've had a credit card since high school and I can promise you between high school and my first few years of working I didn't have much in savings or income. I just managed my debt responsibly. If I couldn't afford it I couldn't afford it.

2. Validating checking account balances with credit card accumulation.

You need to look at your credit card like it's your debit card if you're going to use one. Your credit card balances will come out of a checking account one way or another. You should look at your checking account balances with your credit card balances negated. If you have $1,000 in your checking account and $200 in credit card balances you should look at it as if you only have $800 in there. I promise the credit card balance is not going to magically disappear. Check your credit card balances every week across your checking account to see if you are meeting your budget goals and whether you can afford the balance. If you cannot afford it don't buy it.

I would highly recommend to just set your credit cards to autopay and payoff your statement balance every month. Your credit card can be your friend if you pay off your statement balance every month. If you don't over time interest will become your worst enemy. If you have an emergency use your emergency fund to cover you during your hardship. If you don't have an emergency fund establish that ASAP.

3. Building your credit

Paying off your statement balance every month will also help you build your credit. You will need good credit down the road for bigger loans in your life – when you want to buy a car, a home, or even start your own business. Unless you're paying in cash, you'll need a loan with the best interest rate you can find so you pay less interest during the life of the loan. In order to do this, you'll need a great credit score.

If you've never checked your credit before I'd highly advise to make a free account at creditkarma.com and check your file. It helps to detect identify fraud, debt, active loans, and more. You could be a victim of identity fraud and/or have debt you didn't even know you had.

4. Annual Fees

Avoid credit cards that have annual fees unless they provide you with ample benefit in which you will take advantage. I have two credit cards with annual fees – I have had them for many years. I keep them because the points received for purchases, extra benefits and protection it gives me outweigh the cost of the annual fee. You should feel like you're getting more out of your credit card than the annual fee every year. There should be a ROI for the annual fee you're paying – if not then maybe it's not for you.

These next few tips are inclusive of the main benefits of credit cards. If you're able to follow the previous tips about credit card responsibility then you'll be able to fully juice out the rewards of credit cards to its maximum. A credit card company's main source of profit is customers paying them interest and credit card fees they charge to merchants. You want to be the one profiting off the credit card companies – not them profiting off you. That is the only way this arrangement makes the most sense.

5. Earning and using credit card points

   Points are key to maximizing the value of your credit card. You want credit cards that give you the highest number of points for your purchases. The industry standard for credit cards is to give 1% back in cash or points. When researching credit cards you want to take a look at which categories give more than 1% back in cash or points. For instance, if you eat at restaurants a lot then a card that gives you more points for restaurant purchases would be wise. If you spend more on groceries and eat at home find one that gives you money back for grocery purchases.

   Accumulating points are important because they can generally be used in a variety of ways. They can be used as cash back, buying down your statement balance or (my favorite) vacations/travel. Over the past five years every vacation I've taken has had either free/discounted flights or hotel stays because I was able to utilize the points I accumulated from my credit card purchases. Bigger names in the industry like American Express, Chase, Capital One and more allow consumers to transfer points to use with their specified hotel or airfare partners. This can provide even more benefit depending on the situation. Play the system and enjoy the benefits. Playas don't get played.

6. New Credit Card Bonuses

Generally, when you open up a new credit card they offer new card member bonuses. These vary throughout the year, but keep a look out for these bonuses as they can provide a boost to your bank of points. You'll generally have to spend a certain amount within a certain timeframe to be rewarded for these points. Plan accordingly. For example, if you have a wedding coming up look out for these bonuses – the points may help you pay for some or all of your honeymoon airfare/hotel. The point bonuses I received from wedding spend easily covered our honeymoon flight to Italy. Other events like buying a house (furniture/etc) or having a kid also apply in this situation. These events can be expensive and new credit card bonuses can help with the expense if used correctly.

Beware of the annual fees of some of these credit cards – they can be high. If you pay the annual fee one year and don't want to pay it the next most credit card companies allow you to skip the fee or downgrade the card to a no annual fee card within their base if you threaten to cancel (gray area).

7. Consumer Protections

The last tip is pretty underrated – consumer protections of credit cards. Every card offers different protections, but one of the best protections most credit cards offer is protection against fraud. If your debit card or cash gets stolen and someone uses it your protection is limited. All you can do is call the police and pray for a miracle.

With credit cards you call up your credit card company and tell them your card was stolen or that you did not authorize the transaction. They will validate by contacting the merchant and if your claim is accurate you will get your money back. This is one of the key reasons why middle class income individuals and higher mainly use credit cards for their purchases. In fact, per a Federal Reserve survey in 2022 over 98% of families with over $100,000 in income annually or higher have credit cards. This drops as annual income decreases – as seen in the chart below only 57% of those making less than $25,000 annually had credit

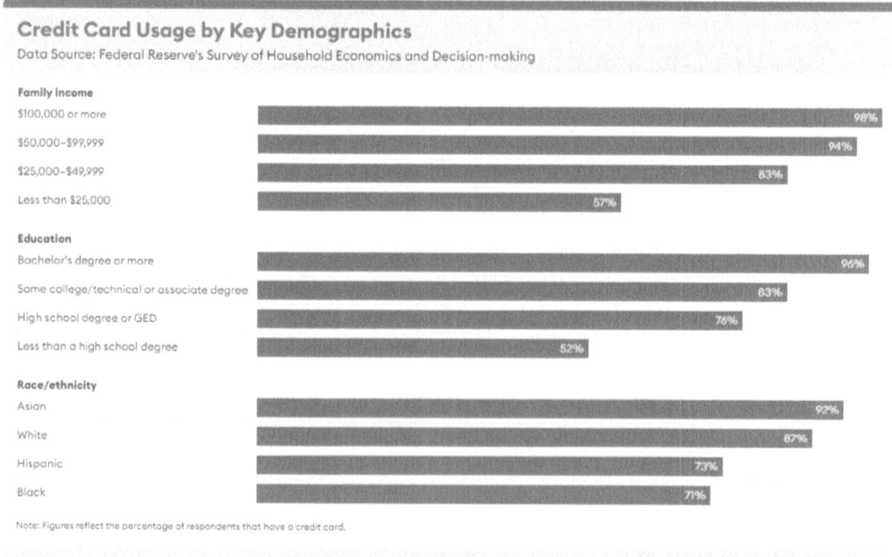

cards[30].

If you have thousands saved on your debit card it's not advisable to carry it around too much – if it gets stolen by the wrong person your whole account could be wiped out in hours. Nowadays online money transfer options like Zelle, CashApp, and Venmo all offer transfer services through your phone. Credit cards offer better protection as long as they're used responsibly. Credit cards also offer additional protections as well such as trip cancellation insurance, rental car insurance, extended warranty, and even cell phone protections depending on the card. Do your research and choose wisely.

8

RELATIONSHIPS

You may be able to get a good college degree, have a fantastic job and achieve FIRE before your 60s, but what's the point if you have toxic relationships with family, friends, or your partner? Maintaining solid relationships is a key to success for your mental wellbeing. At some point in your life, you may think you have it all together and you don't need anyone, but you couldn't be farther from the truth. You always need someone.

Family

Relationships with family can be toxic at times, but at the end of the day they're your family. Imagine there's a zombie apocalypse and you need shelter. Who are most going to call first? Your good ole pal Zack? Hell no! You'll naturally call your immediate family to see if they're okay and figure out shelter plans together. No matter the relationship with your parents/siblings you should always try to have their back. The most important relationship you will ever have is with your family—and you must never forget that.

The exception to this would be if a family member is unreliable and keeps screwing you over. For example, you sign an apartment lease with your brother and he decides to not pay rent and mooch off of you out of sheer laziness. Your parents open up credit cards in your name as a child and never pay them off setting you up with horrible credit. Your sibling sleeps with your significant other (or tries to). Some situations are so messed up that you simply can't ever come back from it. When the level of toxicity reaches a level that's unforgivable it may be wiser to focus on other relationships.

Random Tip: if you have kids it will be helpful to have your parents there to assist. Babysitting, nannies and daycare is expensive and if they like you enough they'll do it for free. Trusted and reliable childcare is gold when you're a parent. Honestly you'll respect your parents a heck of a lot more once you have to raise kids of your own.

Friends

You'll have friends in high school, college, and throughout your post-graduate careers, but will they all be the same people? Most likely the answer to that question would be a no. As you traverse through life and get ahead, you'll find that you're continuously making new friends and trying here and there to catch up with old ones. That is because everyone's journey is different and the phases of life your friends are in likely will not sync up with the phases you're in. For example, even if you go to the same college as your high school bestie, what are the odds that you're in the same major? That you'll go work in the same city after college? Get married and have kids the same year? Astronomically small.

My advice here is not to ditch your old friends or cut them off. Stay in touch, but if they're not on a similar path as you are, don't be afraid to make new friends.

My more prescriptive recommendation is to make friends with people who are in similar circumstances as you or in a circumstance you want to be in. For example, you want to bounce ideas around on whether you're investing your money correctly or if the real estate market is currently in a buyer's market or a seller's market. Would you go ask your buddy Zack from high school who didn't graduate and is working part-time at a fast-food restaurant? Probably not - you'd ask someone who's in a similar boat or someone who's wealthier than you and has been there done that. You want to surround yourself with people who have similar ideals and aspirations for success. Build relationships with these types of people before you need help, not after. The company you keep can influence you in many directions and it's important to keep those with positive energy around you. A person's energy is contagious and people that are negative Nancys or that complain all the time can spread that negativity to you.

If you're truly a winner and winning at life, Zack should be coming to you and asking for advice on how to be successful. As you get older you'll realize that your free time gets more and more limited—especially if you start getting promoted to leadership roles at work, get married or have kids. Do you want to spend that limited free time around friends who don't have similar aspirations for success like you do? Here and there you'll have friends who you just enjoy seeing, but if you feel like you're losing brain cells by hanging out with someone maybe it wouldn't be wise to hang out with them often. Your time is a valuable commodity—spend it wisely.

Finding a Spouse

This will probably be one of the more important relationships you have throughout your life. You'll be spending a lot of time with your partner. Finding this person won't be easy, but if you find the right one all that work will be worth it.

Here are nine tips to find your partner:

1. Finding a good partner who matches your energy, understands you, and has their shit together is a part time job. You'll have to put in the effort, invest in the relationship and go on dates.
2. Don't be discouraged from the fear of failure. Per Wayne Gretzsky "You miss every shot you don't take". Take action and maybe you'll actually get some.
3. If you just got out of a relationship please make sure you're mentally in a good place to find love again before you go on another date. If you meet the right person, but you're not there emotionally you may be wasting a good match.
4. You probably won't find your partner showing up at a random club or bar. I know people who have but can only count the amount on one hand.
5. Don't be afraid of using a dating app. Nowadays it's a norm to meet people on a dating app and it's where I met my wife. We were on dating apps for multiple years before we matched with each other, We went through many bad eggs before we actually found each other. Avoid Tinder. Watch out for the eggplants, peaches, cherries and droplets. IYKYK
6. If dating apps aren't working, go to events and meet new people. Find other singles you are friends with and hit up some social clubs, charity events, or even church events. If you find someone attractive at the grocery store 'accidentally' run into their cart (gently), smile and apologize. Maybe strike up small talk and see

what vibes you get from the person. Ask your friends if they have any single friends, cousins or siblings that are looking for someone. Swallow your pride and you may be rewarded with a life partner.

7. You'll probably seek dating advice from close friends who are also single or are dating/married. Take the advice of those who are dating/married more seriously than those who are single. There's a reason they're in a relationship—they've had success and found their person.
8. Try to find someone who thinks their health and wellbeing is important and takes care of themselves. You want a partner who's going to be there for the long haul. If they don't take care of themselves on autopilot (without you nagging them) then you'll be much more likely to be taking care of them in retirement instead of spending your retirement going to see the world and doing things you both enjoy. They don't need to be an Olympic athlete or have a strict regimen. Your partner should want to take care of their physical and mental health for themselves and not just for you.
9. Follow your intuition. If you have a small voice in your head telling you to choose differently, take it into consideration. Fear can sometimes be disguised or confused as intuition as well. Over time, you'll need to learn the difference to guide you in the right direction. I've encountered many friends in my life who failed to follow their intuition and it led to a tough breakup or divorce. If the fish smells funky don't eat it.

Important Characteristics of a Prospective Life Partner

Your partner should bring you peace. When you end your workday and you see or talk to that person you should naturally feel relieved and happy to see them. If you feel stressed consistently or feel that it's a chore to talk to them after work, you may need to re-evaluate your relationship or work through it with your partner. You should both naturally be happy to talk to each other on the daily after work; if you are in a committed relationship it could be like that for life. You don't want to be stuck in an unhappy relationship long-term. If there are issues like this, fix them before you get too serious.

After you figure each other out the stress should reduce, but when it comes to big life decisions there will likely be arguments. How do you know whether that person will be your peace long-term? A good indicator is the time period between when you start dating and when you get engaged.

After engagement there comes planning a wedding, family relationships, and potentially having children. Those events after engagement can be very stressful and you should expect some fights/arguments during those phases on how you want to make these events happen. That's normal. Once you get through each big phase your relationship should start to normalize and your partner should slowly start to become your peace again. If your partner argues with you a lot pre-engagement and you don't see eye to eye on simpler things, you both either still need to figure things out or this is just the way your relationship will be going forward. Or maybe you're just not right for each other. Simply getting married won't resolve your existing issues; you need to work through them together before marriage.

Another good indicator is if the person shares the same values, mentality, similarities and you're both on the same wavelength. How you both see finances is also very important. If one is a super spender and one is a super saver you may need to work through how you're going to manage your finances long-term. Financial issues are a key reason why people get divorced – you want to shore that up before you get married.

On a more positive note - your partner should end up being one of your best friends. There should be attraction, romance and laughs, but since you'll be spending most of your life with your partner they should understand you, have your back and support you through all endeavors in life. Your spouse should be your number one cheerleader. You should also be their number one cheerleader. Once you start competing and comparing with each other it's a recipe for constant arguments and distrust in the relationship. The both of your successes and failures are both of your successes and failures. Own it and tackle your problems together. Your relationship will likely be happier if your lifelong partner is also your best friend.

9

MENTAL WELLBEING

If there's only one thing you learn from reading this book please let this be the one. If you're not okay mentally the rest of what you need to complete in this book is baloney.

Poor mental health will set you back consistently during key moments in your life (college, jobs, relationships and more). Nothing and I mean absolutely NOTHING is worth compromising your mental health. No issues relating to your relationship partner, school, family, or friendship issues should get in the way of you being okay mentally. Some strategies to help with the 'mentals' (Gen Z Slang) are listed below:

<u>Physical Activity</u>

Go to the gym or join a workout studio. Your physical and mental health are both interconnected and intricate. Engaging in regular exercises releases endorphins from your brain which should improve mental alertness or mood[22]. When I had a tough time with a professor or bad boss I would honestly go hit a punching bag. Imagine the perpetrator's face on the bag and you'll be there longer than expected! It's not a long-term solution, but physical activity did improve my level of optimism and mood when times were tough.

In some of my toughest and most stressful phases of life I would also do Yoga about twice a week. It does not matter what physical condition you're in, everyone can use some yoga to de-stress and decompress from the stresses of life. Turn off your phone during class and focus on what's really important to you at that point in time. Once you learn the poses you can focus on your mental state of being as well during class. Yoga can get expensive so try to find some donation-based yoga studios. You don't need a membership and you can donate whatever you please to the studio for the class.

Physical activity worked for me, but find what you enjoy and helps you decompress from the stresses of life.

What Doesn't Help

Drugs (Including alcohol) doesn't help the situation. It's become a cultural norm to not consider alcohol a drug, but alcohol is a drug and something in which many people have an addiction. The addiction has been normalized by clever marketing and manipulative lobbying by the companies who sell the product. When your mental health is at risk doing any drugs whatsoever doesn't help the situation.

Mindsets, Help and Social Media

Surround yourself with people who have a positive mindset and are optimistic about life. Negative people who constantly bicker and complain all the time can spread their negativity towards you. Negativity and positivity are both contagious in their own ways. Choose to be happy and spread positivity where you can.

Don't be afraid to ask someone for help if things get too serious. Most people who survive suicide attempts have instant regret right as they try to take their own life. Don't let it get to that point and seek help if you're even thinking about something like that. Life is too precious – do what you need to do in order to keep yourself happy. Remember – if can always get worse. Think about those in third world countries who can barely find water to drink on a daily basis. Realign your perspective and appreciate what you have in this life.

Social media can provide positive experiences, but it can also provide a false viewpoint of how life actually is in the real world. Think about it – how often do people actually post what they're actually going through vs what's appealing to people on Instagram so they can get more likes? The real world is not peaches and daisies and just travelling/partying every weekend. Take social media with a grain of salt – many photos have filters and photoshop to alter your perspective on how If you want to take a shot on entrepreneurship hat person's life is truly lived. Take time to detox from social media occasionally and meet up with people in person.

10

ENTREPRENEURSHIP

I spent some time in the startup world as CEO of a small business. I was in the backseat of an Uber at 2am in the drive through of a Whataburger. The idea hit me like lightning and after I was dropped home I couldn't sleep for the next two hours. I had promised myself that when an idea came to my attention I had to write it down. Too many times an idea would pop into my head and I'd forget it moving on to the next idea. I finished my ideation for the night at 4am and woke up the next morning to find my favorite Whataburger honey butter chicken biscuit left uneaten on the kitchen counter.

The next two years were spent ideating, building and creating the business idea and mobile application from scratch. I couldn't afford to leave my day job and pursue this full time as the business was not profitable; I'm very glad I didn't. I would work my eight hours during the day and then have my third dose of coffee at 5pm. While all my friends were talking about the latest Netflix season of Stranger Things, I was sacrificing my short-term happiness for a dream.

I bootstrapped the startup costs with my co-founder and spent about four years ideating and building a mobile app with him. We gained funding and paid registration fees for a swanky apartment in Austin, TX to concentrate fully on the startup together 24/7. We were ready for a hard launch of the mobile app until he accidentally had a launch of his own and got his girlfriend pregnant. My co-founder is also one of my closest friends, so I was ecstatic for him and I did my best to accommodate his wishes.

In 2020 our funding was pulled due to COVID and a few months later I met the love of my life, Zoya. At that point my co-founder and I decided to focus more on stable and less risky income at large corporations until we could regroup and restart our startup journey. Then came engagement, marriage, and a kid of our own a few years later.

The regroup never happened.

My co-founder and I literally endured blood, sweat and tears to build our idea into a product. While we faced failure for many reasons, I can tell you that the knowledge we gained during this time was just as valuable as our startup. The confidence I gained and my learnings about how to run a business has been paramount to my success in the consulting world. It has given me the know-how to relate more with our client's business leaders and has allowed me to spin the failure we endured into a positive investment in myself.

It's pretty much common knowledge to note that most startups fail. In fact, more than 80% of startups fail within the first year according to the Small Business Administration[23]. That's not to detract you from entrepreneurship—honestly the learnings you gain from going down that path (successful or not) are life changing.

During this entire time though, I never left my day job. I had to commit myself to the startup and my day job which took a lot of personal time out of my day. I would advise:

- If you're going down this path don't leave your day job unless you have enough revenue to sustain employment salary for yourself within the organization.
- Try to take on this journey earlier in your life (20s and 30s)

instead of later on in life. When you get into a serious relationship and the marriage discussions begin you'll start to realize you can't be taking as much risk anymore. A steady paycheck will eventually be more appealing to support a family. An ideal time to take higher risk with a startup is when you're younger and single/casually dating around. You'll have more sweat equity to give into the business as time will be an asset.

- If you come up with a great idea, be wary of who you share it with. Snakes come in all shapes and sizes.
- Sacrifice is the name of the game here. Entrepreneurship is like trying to play whack a mole with no moles popping up for you to whack. You have to convince the moles to rise so you can whack them.
- Start your path onto entrepreneurship by starting it as a side hustle to see if you can sustain profitability. Some side hustles can take years to become profitable. If you take a loss and you have a day job you can deduct your losses off of your taxes in most cases.

If you end up taking this path at some point in your life it may be the toughest thing you'll ever do. Whether you succeed or fail, what you learn from the adventure may be the most valuable nugget you receive from the experience.

11

EVERYTHING IS YOUR FAULT

The most profound advice I've ever received is also the most controversial the first time you hear it.

Everything is your fault if you're any damn good (Ernest Hemingway)[29].

When first heard most go straight into the defensive. That's completely normal and understandable. Let me explain 😊

Let’s say you have your own business and you’re the CEO. You’re responsible for the business and all employees succeeding along with making customers happy. You have a successful year in 2024 and smash all expectations. Who gets most of the credit for the successful year? The one who’s leading the effort - the CEO of the company. You.

In 2025 you have a year completely opposite of your year in 2024. You’ve had to layoff 20% of employees, you’re not making a profit and employee morale is at an all time low. Who’s responsible for the bad year? The one who’s running the show – the CEO. You.

No matter how good or bad the company is doing the CEO receives the blame or praise. In the same vein you are the CEO of your own life. Everything you do and every decision you make is of your own choosing. When you’re successful it’s your fault. When you fail it’s also your fault.

It's a lot easier to go along in life pushing the blame for your failures onto the government, your friends, your ex, your family, or other people/things. This makes it much less likely that you’ll actually learn from your failures and fail forward. It shouldn’t be when you succeed you praise yourself, but when you fail you point the finger at others. Set yourself accountable for your actions. This will give you a better opportunity to take action towards your failures and get better.

I'm a big believer in the concept that everyone is dealt a hand in life. It's what you actually do with the hand you were dealt that makes you successful. For those of you who play poker just because you have pocket aces doesn't mean you'll automatically win. You may have the best hand, but you have to play your hand and your opponent right or you'll end up with nothing.

If you were the victim of a crime or action by someone else that's caused you physical or mental issues that's definitely not your fault. I would never insinuate that and hope for you to have a speedy recovery. If you need help mentally see a psychologist. At some point though you can't let your perpetrator live rent free in your head. Do what's necessary to overcome any mental issues caused by this because it will linger and potentially cause issues for you down the road.

You can't always control someone else's ability to harm you, but you can control what you do after the event. Seek justice, mental resolution, and either own it or let it go. This could honestly take years depending on the severity of the issue. Don't let the crime be the reason why you weren't successful. Don't let it be a crutch that holds you back. Persevere and be stronger. See a mental health professional if needed and take control of your issues.

I've met hundreds of rich and poor people. Some of them had

wealthy parents growing up, but now they're about middle class or poor. Some families made good decisions and kept themselves wealthy. The wealthiest man I know also at one point in the past was the poorest man I knew.

He did not grow up wealthy. He was so poor he used to get a McDouble from the dollar menu at McDonalds, cut the burger into fourths and split it as his four meals for the day while chugging water to keep himself satiated. He now owns multiple businesses and makes a doctor's annual salary every month at the minimum. You can start off poor, sacrifice, work hard and become rich. You can also start off rich, get greedy and lose part or all of your wealth. You can also start off in the middle class and stay there.

Wealthy or poor everyone has their own set of challenges in life to go through. Until you live life in their shoes try your best not to judge someone else's situation. You are the CEO of your own life – you should want the best for yourself and your loved ones. Put your best foot forward for YOU.

10

CLOSING THOUGHTS

Success in life comes in many shapes and sizes. Your perspective of success could be having a family, achieving financial success, or traveling our beautiful world. Your perspective of success may also change over the course of your life as you achieve certain goals.

The chapters outlined in this book were written to give you the knowledge (with no **BS**) to evade pitfalls you may fall into during life as a young adult. You'll be trying and doing many things for the first time; it's important to prepare you for what school does not. I hope you were able to take at least one nugget of knowledge from this book to help you traverse your upcoming journey in life. Make your decisions with confidence after doing your research and be all you can be. Believe in yourself even if no one else believes in you. One day someone will.

The reason for focusing on specific decision points early on in your adulthood is because adulting in the long-term can become a LOT harder if you don't make the right decisions in high school, college and your first 5-10 years on the job.

For instance, if you don't contribute to a 401k until your 40s or 50s with no alternative retirement plan, trying to catch up is very expensive. These decisions will set you up for success financially and in life and for the long-term.

Continue seeking knowledge from a variety of topics and enrich your mind. Learning is a lifelong journey and can come in many different formats. If you've never traveled to a third world country please book the flight when the time is right. You'll never truly appreciate what you have until you see how many billions are living without the basic necessities we live with today. Once you're successful, give back to those who need support or on their journey to success. Be someone's mentor and pass the learnings forward.

Best of luck on your journey of life. I hope you'll never need it.

Hard Work > Luck.

P.S.
If you enjoyed this book please take a moment to provide a review on Amazon and Goodreads in order to spread the knowledge forward. Any feedback would be appreciated.

Thank you for reading and your support!

Bibliography

1. Punjwani. "Average Salary in the U.S. in 2024" https://www.usatoday.com/money/blueprint/business/hr-payroll/average-salary-us/

2. Hermann, A., and Whitney, P. "Home price-to-income ratio reaches record high". Joint Center for Housing Studies of Harvard University, January 22, 2024. https://www.jchs.harvard.edu/blog/home-price-income-ratio-reaches-record-high-0, accessed June 24, 2024.

3. https://utulsa.edu/news/normalizing-the-norm-of-changing-college-majors/, accessed June 24, 2024.

4. Hanson, Melanie. "Average Medical School Debt" EducationData.org, September 17, 2023, https://educationdata.org/average-medical-school-debt, accessed June 24, 2024.

5. Med School Insiders. "US Medical School Dropout Rates & Why Students Drop Out", August 28, 2023, https://medschoolinsiders.com/pre-med/medical-school-dropout-rates/, accessed June 24, 2024.

6. Salary.com. "First Year Medical Resident Salary in the United States". https://www.salary.com/research/salary/hiring/first-year-medical-resident-salary, accessed July 2, 2024.
7. Mercer Caroline. "How work hours affect medical resident performance and wellness". *CMAJ.* 2019 Sep 30;191(39):E1086-E1087. https://www.ncbi.nlm.nih.gov/pmc/articles/PMC6773545/, accessed July 2, 2024.
8. Murphy, Brendan. "6 things medical students should know

about physician compensation". American Medical Association, https://www.ama-assn.org/medical-students/specialty-profiles/6-things-medical-students-should-know-about-physician, accessed July 2, 2024.

9. Murphy, Brendan. "How often do physicians and medical students die of suicide?" American Medical Association, June 12, 2019. https://www.ama-assn.org/practice-management/physician-health/how-often-do-physicians-and-medical-students-die-suicide, accessed June 24, 2024.

10. Gailey, Alex. *Nearly 80% of graduates with the 20 most lucrative college degrees are men* Bankrate. September 5th 2023 https://www.bankrate.com/loans/student-loans/top-paying-college-majors-gender-gap/ accessed July 5th, 2024.

11. Hanson, Melanie. "Average Private vs Public College Tuition". Education Data Initiative, October 22, 2023. https://educationdata.org/private-vs-public-college-tuition, accessed June 24, 2024.

12. Weiss, Marc. "An Aid to Adapting: Adopting the 70% Rule". ManagementONE.https://www.management-one.com/blog/an-aid-to-adapting-adopting-the-70-percent-rule#:~:text=One%20way%20to%20manage%20this,stress%20yourself%20out%20even%20more, accessed June 24, 2024.

13. University of Southern California. "Studying for Finals? Let Classical Music Help". https://today.usc.edu/studying-for-finals-let-classical-music-help/, accessed July 2, 2024.

14. Myers, Sydney. "2023 Applicant Tracking System (ATS) Usage Report: Key Shifts and Strategies for Job Seekers". Jobscan, October 2,

2023. https://www.jobscan.co/blog/fortune-500-use-applicant-tracking-systems/, accessed July 2, 2024.

15. Kurter, Heidi "6 Recruiter Tips To Getting Your Resume Seen And Landing An Interview". October 15th 2020 https://www.forbes.com/sites/heidilynnekurter/2020/10/13/6-recruiter-tips-to-getting-your-resume-seen-and-landing-an-interview/ , accessed July 5th 2024

16. Kenton, Will. " S&P 500 Index: What It's for and Why It's Important in Investing". Investopedia, June 12, 2024. https://www.investopedia.com/terms/s/sp500.asp, accessed July 2, 2024.
17. Bankrate. "401K Retirement Calculator". https://www.bankrate.com/retirement/401-k-calculator/, accessed July 2, 2024.

18. Maverick, J.B. "S&P 500 Average Return and Historical Performance" Investopedia, January 3, 2024. https://www.investopedia.com/ask/answers/042415/what-average-annual-return-sp-500.asp, accessed July 2, 2024.

19. Floyd, David. "Buffett's Bet with the Hedge Funds: And the Winner Is …" Investopedia, June 25, 2019. https://www.investopedia.com/articles/investing/030916/buffetts-bet-hedge-funds-year-eight-brka-brkb.asp, accessed July 2, 2024.

20. Charles Schwab. "Why diversification matters". https://www.schwab.com/learn/story/why-diversification-matters, accessed July 2, 2024.

21. Perez, Lauren. "What Is the Average Interest Rate for Savings Accounts?". Smartasset, June 18, 2024.

https://smartasset.com/checking-account/average-savings-account-interest, accessed July 2, 2024.

22. Priory. "How exercise benefits mental health". https://www.priorygroup.com/blog/exercise-to-improve-mental-health, accessed June 24, 2024.

23. Bryant, Sean. "How Many Startups Fail and Why?" *Investopedia,* November 26, 2022. https://www.investopedia.com/articles/personal-finance/040915/how-many-startups-fail-and-why.asp, accessed June 24, 2024.

24. DeVonne, Cheyenne. "Here's how much money Americans in their 30s have in their 401(k)s". *CNBC*, March 23, 2024. https://www.cnbc.com/2024/03/23/how-much-money-americans-in-their-30s-have-in-their-401ks.html, accessed June 24, 2024.

25. Elder, Grace. "Five benefits of journaling". *The Journal Rewired,* November 15, 2021. https://thejournalrewired.com/21509/showcase/five-bennifits-of-journaling/ accessed June 24, 2024.

26. Mirza AA., Baig M., Beyari GM., Halawani MA., Mirza AA. "Depression and Anxiety Among Medical Students: A Brief Overview". *Adv Med Educ Pract*. 2021 Apr 21;12:393-398. doi: 10.2147/AMEP.S302897. PMID: 33911913; PMCID: PMC8071692. https://www.ncbi.nlm.nih.gov/pmc/articles/PMC8071692/#:~:text=The%20estimated%20frequency%20of%20depression,systematic%20review%20and%20meta%2Danalysis.&text=Another%20systematic%20review%20found%20that,varied%20between%206.0%E2%80%9366.5%25, accessed June 24,

2024.

27. Raisinghani, Vishesh "Dave Ramsey says 'very few people' who look like they have money actually do — claims vastly expensive cars, vacations on social media are rarely signs of real wealth. Here's the true test" July 11th 2024. https://moneywise.com/life/lifestyle/dave-ramseys-true-test-of-wealth
28. https://www.azquotes.com/quote/1445266, accessed July 23rd 2024
29. JT Genter "Why Dave Ramsey is Both Right and Wrong on Credit Cards" https://thepointsguy.com/credit-cards/dave-ramsey-right-wrong-credit-cards/ March 6, 2018
30. Pokora, Becky "Credit Card Statistics and Trends 2024" https://www.forbes.com/advisor/credit-cards/credit-card-statistics/ March 28th 2024
31. Woolsey, Ben "Average Credit Card Interest Rate for July 2024: 24.72% APR" https://www.investopedia.com/average-credit-card-interest-rate-5076674 July 2nd 2024

www.ingramcontent.com/pod-product-compliance
Ingram Content Group UK Ltd.
Pitfield, Milton Keynes, MK11 3LW, UK
UKHW041852190726
13854UKWH00002B/859